GUIDE FOR
LITURGY COMMITTEES

SECOND EDITION

Corinna Laughlin

Michael R. Prendergast

Joanne Sanders

Paul Turner

LITURGY
TRAINING
PUBLICATIONS

Nihil Obstat   *Imprimatur*
Rev. Mr. Daniel G. Welter, JD   Most Rev. Robert G. Casey
Chancellor   Vicar General
Archdiocese of Chicago   Archdiocese of Chicago
May 26, 2021   May 26, 2021

The Glossary definitions and portions of the Resources section were written by Dennis C. Smolarski, SJ, and Joseph DeGrocco. Additional questions for discussion and reflection provided by Mary G. Fox and Lorie Simmons.

Cover photo © Liturgy Training Publications. Interior photos on pages 15, 20, 27, 28, 33, 38, 47, and 50 © Liturgy Training Publications; pages 3, 5, 13, 21, 42, 43, and 54 by John Zich.

GUIDE FOR LITURGY COMMITTEES, SECOND EDITION © 2021 Archdiocese of Chicago: Liturgy Training Publications, 3949 South Racine Avenue, Chicago, IL 60609; 800-933-1800; fax: 800-933-7094, email: orders@ltp.org; website: www.LTP.org. All rights reserved.

This book is part of the Liturgical Ministry Series®.

This book was edited by Danielle A. Noe. Michael A. Dodd was the production editor, Anna Manhart was the designer, and Kari Nicholls was the production artist.

25 24 23 22 21   1 2 3 4 5

Printed in the United States of America

Library of Congress Control Number: 2021936117

ISBN: 978-1-61671-586-1

ELMLC2

Contents

❦

Preface   *iv*

How to Use This Resource   *vii*

Chapter One
Your Ministry and the Liturgy   1

Chapter Two
The Meaning and History of Your Ministry   7

Chapter Three
Serving on the Liturgy Committee   19

Chapter Four
Spirituality and Discipleship   36

Chapter Five
Frequently Asked Questions   47

Resources   *61*

Glossary   *65*

Prayer for Liturgy Committees   *80*

Preface

"Master, we have worked hard all night and have caught nothing,
but at your command I will lower the nets."

—Luke 5:5

S imon had prepared everything perfectly. Two boats rested at the shore. Andrew, James, and John were finishing dinner at their homes. They were gathering up stories and laughter, skills and tools. Soon they would all rendezvous at the lake to do what they had practiced, performed, and enjoyed all their lives. They were going fishing.

Simon was bringing a new net. He was especially proud of it. Tight and strong, it seemed even more anxious for work than he was. He hoisted it like a trophy and shook it in triumph. "You'll have fresh fish for breakfast," he promised his wife. She smiled and kissed him. He strode out the door.

Simon was a natural leader. He provided for his family. He made friends easily. People respected his knowledge of the sea, his organizational skills, and his way with words. They gladly followed his directions, and they let him speak on their behalf.

Celebration filled the air as night fell over the waters. Simon and his companions leaped into the boats and pushed out into the deep. The moment had arrived. Simon got the attention of his friends; then he tossed his new net into the lake and hauled it back toward the boat.

Nothing. Andrew cocked an eyebrow. Simon shrugged and tossed again. John helped him pull the net back this time.

Nothing again. They both looked perplexed. Something was wrong. Just for the sheer novelty of the idea, they tossed the new net to the other side of the boat and hauled it in. Empty.

Simon sat down. The conversation became as still as the sea. Simon ran back through his mental checklist. He had planned everything just right: He brought his tools. He navigated to the right location. The proper hour for fishing had arrived. It was just odd.

"It has to work," he concluded. So he tossed the net again. And again. And again. And again. All night long, Simon and his friends worked as hard as they had ever worked. They had nothing to show for it—absolutely nothing but raw nerves and calloused hands.

Dawn broke. Simon parked his boat on the shore while the others kept trying. He simply could not believe he had failed. He cleaned his new net, not that it needed much attention. After that, he wanted to be alone—away from his friends—before going home.

Excited voices suddenly rose in the distance. Simon's moment of solitude was shattered by a crowd of villagers turning toward the lake. In his morning of embarrassment, Simon did not want an audience. But dozens of people descended upon him, all following a man heading toward the lake.

"Over here," he was saying. "There! There's a boat!" the stranger announced, grinning through his beard, and pointing toward Simon's newly abandoned craft. "Sir," the stranger said to Simon, "Mind if I use your boat?" He stepped in without awaiting a response.

"Lousy time for fishing," Simon said. "And you can't fit this many people in a skiff."

"No, no," the man explained. "I need a place to teach. Push this thing off a bit for me, would you?"

Andrew looked puzzled. Someone from the crowd filled him in: "This is Jesus. We've come to hear the word of God."

Simon was too tired to argue. Besides, he needed something to distract the crowd from his night of failure. He tipped the boat gently toward the water. Jesus sat down in it and spoke. The water amplified the sound of his voice, and everyone heard plainly. Simon had to respect a guy with organizational skills like that. It seemed as though this Jesus had no plan at all, yet he used the people, the tools, and even the landscape to his advantage. The man was a leader. He could speak well. People listened to him.

Simon was still lost in his thoughts when Jesus wrapped up his speech and turned his face toward the failed fisher. "Put out into deep water," he said to Simon. Then he called out to Andrew, James, and John, "and lower your nets for a catch!"[1]

This was too much. Simon was a professional fisher. This guy obviously was not. He was a smooth-tongued philosopher. Simon wanted to show respect, but he didn't need advice. He knew perfectly well how to fish. True, he had no fish at the moment to prove it, but this was his life. Besides, he would now have to admit his failure publicly. Simon tightened his lips and said to Jesus, "Master, we have worked hard all night and have caught nothing." Then, exhausted, trying to save face, he decided to teach the teacher a lesson. "But at your command I will lower the nets."[2]

Jesus smiled, sat back, hands behind his head, and watched.

Simon lifted his clean new net and tossed it into the lake. The water shook beneath the boat. Simon pulled on the net. It wouldn't budge. Andrew helped. Together they strained. To his horror, Simon noticed something. "My new net! It's breaking!" They signaled to their friends in the other boat. "Guys, get over

1. Luke 5:4.
2. Luke 5:5.

here, would you?" It took the force of all of them to haul the fish on board. Sardines, musht, and catfish spilled all over the deck of Simon's boat, flopping in loud celebration and covering Jesus up to his hips.

The boat began to sink under the weight of the fish. Simon's net was torn, and now he was in danger of losing his boat. He fell to his knees, fish slapping at his thighs. He didn't feel like much of a leader, but he raised his voice above the din and gave Jesus a command. "Depart from me, Lord, for I am a sinful man."[3]

But Jesus had another plan. He spoke to the man who thought he had it all organized: his boat, his net, his friends, and his life. Jesus said something that caused Simon to give it all up at once: "Do not be afraid."[4]

Simon and his friends reached the shore, where they abandoned their boat and their nets, their skills and their know-how. They didn't need them anymore. They would no longer catch fish. They would catch people. Jesus had a plan. Now they had to prepare for it.

—Paul Turner

---

3. Luke 5:8.
4. Luke 5:10.

How to Use This Resource

A liturgy committee helps prepare a community to carry out the Church's plan of worship. The members represent different areas of expertise. They come to a meeting ready to put their knowledge and skills to work for the sake of others. As with any committee work, there is always a little give and take. Sometimes the members work hard and have little to show for it. Usually, the results are not quite what any individual had in mind. The goal is to do what God has in mind. The goal is to discern the prompting of the Holy Spirit.

This book will help you understand the work of the liturgy committee, and where you and your skills fit. It will explain what the liturgy is about and how liturgy committees came to be. It will offer you spiritual reflection on the gifts God has given you, and it will answer your practical questions.

About the Authors

Corinna Laughlin is the pastoral assistant for liturgy at St. James Cathedral in Seattle, Washington, and liturgy consultant for the Archdiocese of Seattle. She has written extensively on the liturgy for Liturgy Training Publications and has contributed articles to *Pastoral Liturgy*®, *Ministry and Liturgy*, and other publications. She holds a doctorate in English from the University of Washington.

Michael R. Prendergast has nearly fifty years' experience as a musician and liturgist at the parish, cathedral, and diocesan levels. He is the former liturgy specialist and editor of *Today's Liturgy* at Oregon Catholic Press. A native of the Diocese of Helena, Montana, Michael is an adjunct instructor in the departments of theology and music at the University of Portland, Oregon, serves as the coordinator of liturgy and music at St. Andrew Parish in Portland, and is the founder of Sacred Liturgy Ministries, a liturgical consulting firm. Michael has written on topics related to music and liturgy in several liturgical and pastoral journals. He is one of the compilers of LTP's *Pronunciation Guide for the Lectionary: A Comprehensive Resource for Proclaimers of the Word, Second Edition*. He holds a master's in theological studies from Mount Angel Seminary, St. Benedict, Oregon, and a master's in liturgical studies from St. John's University in Collegeville, Minnesota.

Joanne Sanders is the director of worship and Christian initiation for Resurrection Catholic Church, in Wayne, Illinois. She also serves on the Diocesan Liturgy Board for the Diocese of Joliet. A workshop presenter and ministry consultant, she holds a bachelor of arts in psychology from the

University of Illinois and a master of arts in pastoral studies with a concentration in Word and worship from Catholic Theological Union in Chicago. She is the coauthor, with Yvonne Cassa, of *Groundwork: Planning Liturgical Seasons* (LTP) and *How to Form a Parish Liturgy Board* (LTP). Along with Yvonne, she also wrote a liturgy preparation column in *Celebration* for several years. Joanne is a wife, mother, and grandmother; she is indebted to all the liturgy committee members who have been an inspiration to her over the years.

Paul Turner is the pastor of the Cathedral of the Immaculate Conception in Kansas City, Missouri, and the director of the Office of Divine Worship for the Diocese of Kansas City–St. Joseph. He holds a doctorate in sacred theology from Sant'Anselmo in Rome and is the author of many pastoral and theological resources. He serves as a facilitator for the International Commission on English in the Liturgy.

Questions for Discussion and Reflection

1. Why have you agreed to serve on the liturgy committee at your church?

2. What do you hope to gain in your understanding of the theology and function of the ministry through this book?

Chapter One

Your Ministry and the Liturgy

[The liturgy] is the source and summit of the Christian life.
—*Lumen gentium*, 11

You are currently serving your faith community as a member of the liturgy committee or you would like to serve in this way. Your love for Christ draws you to attend Mass. Your love for the Church draws you to liturgical service. Your membership on the liturgy committee is integral to the preparation that is essential for fostering the "full, conscious, and active participation"[1] of everyone who worships in your faith community.

A liturgy committee gives shape to the liturgy, but the liturgy gives shape to the committee members. To serve well requires a good understanding of what liturgy is, how it evolved, and how it stays fresh.

The liturgy is the official prayer of the Church. Through Eucharist, our redemption is accomplished, for when we eat and drink the Body and Blood of the Lord, we are already at table with Christ in the Kingdom of Heaven. Jesus Christ promised that those

> For the liturgy . . . is the outstanding means whereby the faithful may express their lives and manifest to others the mystery of Christ and the real nature of the true Church.
>
> —*Sacrosanctum concilium*, 2

who eat his Body and drink his Blood remain in him and he in them.[2] The liturgy benefits those who celebrate it.

The liturgy also benefits the world. Through it, those who celebrate manifest the mystery of Christ to others. They live according to his teachings and in the life of his Holy Spirit. They also express what the Church is: a human and divine entity, active in the world with prayer and service, yet on pilgrimage to that city yet to come.[3]

You already know the importance of attending and participating at Mass. The Eucharist sums up our beliefs that there is a God, that God's Word took flesh in Christ, that the Holy Spirit continues to guide the Church, that God speaks to us through the Scriptures, that Christ worked miracles, that he gave us his Body and Blood on the night before he died, and that he rose from the

---

1. *Sacrosanctum concilium* (SC), 14. This document is also commonly referred to by its English title, the *Constitution on the Sacred Liturgy*. The paragraphs in Church documents are numbered sequentially. The references throughout this resource refer to the corresponding paragraph numbers in the quoted document. Universal Church documents are usually issued first in Latin. Throughout this resource, the Latin titles of these documents have been used. The English titles refer to those documents that are issued by the United States Conference of Catholic Bishops. Hereafter, in footnotes this document will be abbreviated as SC.
2. See John 6:56.
3. See SC, 2 and Hebrews 13:14.

1

dead on the third day. When we gather for the Eucharist as the Body of Christ, we place our lives in God's hands. We respond in faith to the revelation we have received. You are ministering in the Church as a member of the liturgy committee because one thing is clear: the liturgy matters to you.

What Is Liturgy?

Dictionaries will tell you, in one way or another, that *liturgy* is a collection of rites used in public worship. And that is true. But there is much more to liturgy than that. The word *liturgy* comes from a Greek word meaning "public work" or "work of the people." That hits nearer the mark: liturgy is a special kind of work in which the divine and human come together; we do something, and, more importantly, God does something. Liturgy is not a thing; liturgy is an *event.* So let's ask a different question: What does liturgy *do?*

Liturgy gathers us in the presence of God. In speaking of the Eucharist, the second-century *Didache* emphasizes gathering: "Even as this broken bread was scattered over the hills, and was gathered together and became one, so let Your Church be gathered together from the ends of the earth into Your kingdom."[4] Here the Eucharistic bread, formed from many grains of wheat, is an image of what we are to be: disparate individuals who become something new— a worshiping assembly. In the Bible, the gathering of God's people is a sign of the in-breaking of the kingdom of God. Think of Isaiah's vision of a great banquet on a mountaintop.[5] Think of Jesus feeding the multitudes[6] or of the disciples gathered in prayer in the upper room on the first Pentecost.[7] When God gathers his people together, something happens. The same is true of the liturgy. Before a word has been spoken or a note sung, the liturgy is already a sign of the kingdom of God because it gathers us together.

> In the liturgy, by means of signs perceptible to the senses human sanctification is signified and brought about in ways proper to each of these signs.
>
> —*Sacrosanctum concilium*, 7

Liturgy helps form us into a community. The act of being together at table, of sharing the Word of God, of being one voice in our sung and spoken prayers, has an impact on us. It is through this shared action in the liturgy that we learn to recognize ourselves as a family of believers, the Body of Christ, and to be united in our action outside of the church as well. We join in the liturgy because we are a community, but the reverse is also true: without the liturgy, we are not a community at all.

---

4. *The Didache: The Lord's Teaching Through the Twelve Apostles to the Nations*, 9. http://www.new advent.org/fathers/0714.htm; accessed August 28, 2019.
5. See Isaiah 25:6–9.
6. See Matthew 14:13–21, Mark 6:30–44, Luke 9:10–17, and John 6:1–15.
7. See Acts of the Apostles 2:1–11.

Liturgy is both common and cosmic. The liturgy takes the most ordinary things—our bodies and voices, light and darkness, water and fire, bread, wine, and oil, time itself—and, through the action of the Holy Spirit, transforms all of these into God's very presence. The liturgy teaches us to see that the entire universe is marked with the presence of Christ. The "seeds" of God are everywhere in the world. The stuff of our holiness is not far away, remote, or arcane. The common is holy.

Christian liturgy is always about the paschal mystery. At the heart of all Christian prayer is the paschal mystery—that is, the life, death, and resurrection of Christ. Whether our prayer is the Mass, the Liturgy of the Hours, a saint's day, a sacrament—whether it is Advent or Christmas Time, Lent,

Triduum, or Easter Time—the liturgy is always about the paschal mystery. Why is the paschal mystery so important? Because, in the words of St. Paul, "if Christ has not been raised, your faith is vain; you are still in your sins."[8] The paschal mystery is the fulcrum of history and the dynamic reality which gives meaning to our lives and enlivens our worship. We gather for liturgy in order to be plunged, again and again, into the paschal mystery.

In the liturgy, we meet Christ. We know that Christ is always close to those who believe: Jesus said, "whoever loves me will keep my word, and my Father will love

It is through shared action in the liturgy that we learn to recognize ourselves as a family of believers, the Body of Christ, and to be united in our action outside of the church as well.

him, and we will come to him and make our dwelling with him."[9] But, in the celebration of the Eucharist, Christ is present to us in a special way. In fact, the Church highlights *four* presences of Christ at Mass. Christ is present in the community gathered for prayer; Christ comes to us in each other. Christ is present in the priest, who acts *in persona Christi*, in the person of Christ, in the Mass. Christ is present in the word proclaimed: "When the Sacred Scriptures are read in the Church, God himself speaks to his people, and Christ, present in his word, proclaims the Gospel."[10] And in a unique way, Christ is present in the consecrated bread and wine, his true Body and Blood, shared with us in the Eucharist. Through our participation in this mystery, we meet Christ in many ways and we become what we receive: the Body of Christ.[11]

---

8. I Corinthians 15:17.
9. John 14:23.
10. GIRM, 29.
11. See SC, 7.

Liturgy is the worship of the Church. The liturgy is not free-form. As the official prayer of the universal Church, it is governed by universal norms. Most of the texts we hear at Mass—with some significant exceptions, like the homily and the universal prayer—are written down and are the same the world over. Not only the words of liturgy, but most of the actions are the same everywhere: standing, sitting, and kneeling. The liturgical books include many rubrics (from the Latin word for "red," because these instructions are sometimes printed in red ink), which give instructions for how and where each part of the liturgy happens. All of this should remind us that the liturgy does not belong to any one person, priest, or parish. The liturgy is the Church's prayer. But, that does not mean that it is not *our* prayer too. In the words of the Second Vatican Council, the liturgy is "the outstanding means whereby the faithful may express in their lives and manifest to others the mystery of Christ and the real nature of the true Church."[12] Liturgy is our means of expression with Christ and about Christ. In other words, liturgy is the language we speak as Catholics.

> ———— ✿ ————
> The preeminent manifestation of the Church is present in the full, active participation of all God's holy people in these liturgical celebrations, especially in the same eucharist.
> —*Sacrosanctum concilium*, 41

The liturgy is richly varied. While the liturgy is carefully governed by liturgical books, it is never monotone. It is constantly changing, with different readings for every day of the year, and different prayers for most days. Through the liturgical year, the Church invites us to meditate on different aspects of the mystery of Christ, from his conception to his second coming. The liturgy is colorful!

The Eucharist is the most important of the Church's liturgies, but it is not our only liturgy. The liturgies of the Church also include rites like those in the *Rite of Christian Initiation of Adults*[13] and the *Order of Christian Funerals*. They include celebrations of the other sacraments, from baptism, confirmation, and Eucharist to anointing and penance, matrimony, and holy orders. In addition, the Liturgy of the Hours, prayed daily by deacons, priests, bishops, religious, and many laypeople, is part of the Church's liturgy, sanctifying the hours of each day with prayer to God.

Liturgy is different from devotion. The Church has a rich and wonderful array of devotional prayer—novenas, chaplets, the Rosary, the Way of the Cross, among others—which can enrich our prayer and bring us closer to Christ and to his Mother. The Rosary has a special place in the life of the Church, for, in the words of St. John Paul II, it "serves as an excellent introduction and a faithful echo of the Liturgy, enabling people to participate fully and interiorly

---

12. SC, 2.

13. At the time of this printing, a new translation of the *Rite of Christian Initiation of Adults* is being prepared by the USCCB and pending Vatican approval. The new title of the book will be the *Order of Christian Initiation of Adults*. Check with your pastor or director of liturgy about the status of the new translation.

in it and to reap its fruits in their daily lives."[14] These devotions can enrich, but must never replace, our participation in the liturgy.

Liturgy both reflects and shapes our faith. A medieval scholar expressed this in a phrase that has become famous: *lex orandi, lex credendi*, which can loosely be translated as "the law of prayer shapes the law of belief." In other words, the way we pray informs our theology. If you look at the footnotes in the documents of the Second Vatican Council, and in the *Catechism of the Catholic Church*, you'll notice that the sources cited for key teachings not only include the Bible and teachings of popes and councils, but prayers from the Mass. Liturgy is a school of prayer and a school of faith, teaching us to believe with the Church.

The medieval adage is often extended to read *lex orandi, lex credendi, lex vivendi*—"law of life." The way we pray shapes what we believe—and the way we live our lives. Authentic worship and faith lead to discipleship. If it doesn't, it means the transforming power of the liturgy is not really reaching us. As Pope Benedict XVI has written, "A Eucharist which does not pass over into the concrete practice of love is intrinsically fragmented."[15]

Liturgical prayer reflects what is is Catholics believe and how we are to live in the world.

Liturgy really matters. *Sacrosanctum concilium* of the Second Vatican Council had this to say about liturgy: "The liturgy is the summit toward which the activity of the Church is directed; at the same time it is the font from which all the Church's power flows."[16] Liturgy is both source and summit, culmination and starting-place. All the preaching and evangelizing the Church does is meant to draw people to Christ in the celebration of the Eucharist. At the same time, though, the Eucharist is not a stopping place. Liturgy is the fountain from which we draw strength to do Christ's work in the world. Liturgy gathers us; liturgy also sends us forth. And if liturgy fails to do that, there is a problem. "We cannot delude ourselves," wrote St. John Paul II, "by our mutual love and, in particular, by our concern for those in need we will be recognized as true followers of Christ. . . . This will be the criterion by which the authenticity of our Eucharistic celebrations is judged."[17]

---

14. *Rosarium Virginis Mariae,* 4.
15. *Deus caritas est,* 14.
16. SC, 10.
17. *Mane nobiscum Domine,* 28.

The Privilege to Serve

Liturgical ministers have the wonderful privilege of helping others participate in this transforming reality we call the Church's liturgy. Whether we are proclaiming a Scripture reading, taking up the collection, distributing Communion, carrying a candle, or preparing the liturgical environment, our goal is the same: to help others find in the liturgy what we have found—a community of believers, a school of holiness, a place of encounter with Jesus Christ. When we go to Mass, we never come out the same, because liturgy is meant to change us. No wonder, then, that the Church puts such emphasis on participation in the liturgy. If we participate fully, consciously, and actively in the liturgy, we cannot fail to be transformed, and do our part to transform the world we live in. As liturgical ministers, we are called to do just that, and to help others do the same.

Questions for Reflection and Discussion

1. How is praying with a community different than praying on your own? Why do you think Jesus calls us to pray in both ways?

2. What liturgies of the Church do you participate in on a regular basis?

3. Where and when do you feel closest to Christ?

4. Think about the ways Christ is present in the liturgy and in the world. Think of a time when you have felt Christ's presence in these places.

5. Do you find that participating in the liturgy affects your life outside of the liturgy?

Chapter Two

The Meaning and History of Your Ministry

I received from the Lord what I also handed on to you. . . .
As often as you eat this bread and drink the cup, you
proclaim the death of the Lord until he comes.

—1 Corinthians 11:23, 26

Of all the work the Church does, nothing is more important than Sunday Eucharist. The liturgy "is the source and summit of Christian faith."[1] At the start of the week, Sunday Mass is the source of our strength. It is also the goal toward which our week strives. When we gather for Eucharist, we celebrate all that has been accomplished, and we receive nourishment to do God's will again in the days ahead.

The Church's mission requires the participation of everyone—both in worship and in prayer. The obligation pertaining to Mass on Sunday is not just to attend, but to participate.[2] The Church desires full, conscious, and active participation of the faithful at worship.

Your work on a liturgy committee then fulfills these aims. You will facilitate the participation of the people in the wondrous act of Eucharist. There, as we eat and drink the Body and Blood of the Lord, the work of our redemption is accomplished, we reach the summit of our activity as a Church, and we drink from the fount of the Spirit of Christ.

> The liturgy is the summit toward which the activity of the Church is directed; at the same time it is the fount from which all the Church's power flows.
>
> —*Sacrosanctum concilium*, 10

You will do this not just in your work, but in the attitude you bring to it. As you work in harmony with others, you are already demonstrating the Church at work: the Body of Christ, the parts working together to glorify God and to serve others.

A Baptismal Call

Your desire to serve God in the Church flows from baptism, which is the foundation of all ministry. Before you serve as a liturgical minister or as a member of a committee, you are a baptized member of the Body of Christ, with all the attendant blessings and duties.

---

1. *Lumen gentium* (LG), 11.
2. See *Code of Canon Law*, 1247, 1248.

Baptism helps you personally: it cleanses you from sin and incorporates you into the Body of Christ. Baptism also gives you responsibilities toward others: it assigns you a place among the faithful who worship at the Eucharist and who serve their neighbor in the name of Christ. Baptism summons you to worship and service.

As a believer, your role at Mass is so important that, together with others at church, you are called a priestly people. All the faithful join with the celebrant to give thanks to God and to offer the sacrifice. In doing this, they also learn to offer themselves completely to God.[3] The law about going to Mass on Sunday is not to "attend" Mass, but to *participate* at Mass.[4] All the baptized have something to do there. It is not just the priest who offers—all the priestly people offer themselves, offer the sacrifice, and share the communion.

We become a priestly people at baptism. During the liturgy, a child is anointed on the crown of the head with chrism, while the priest or deacon says:

> Almighty God, the Father of our Lord Jesus Christ,
> has freed you from sin,
> given you new birth by water and the Holy Spirit,
> and joined you to his people.
> He now anoints you with the Chrism of salvation,
> so that you may remain members of Christ, Priest,
> > Prophet and King,
> unto eternal life.[5]

Christians are anointed into the ministry of Christ as leaders. Our participation at Mass is priestly: "The faithful indeed, by virtue of their royal priesthood, share in the offering of the Eucharist."[6] They do so in other ways as well: "They exercise that priesthood, too, by the reception of the sacraments, by prayer and thanksgiving, by the witness of a holy life, self-denial and active charity."[7]

Baptism seals us for worship and marks us as children of God. Because it is received only once, Baptism imparts a special character for this purpose: "Incorporated into the church by Baptism, the faithful are appointed by their baptismal character to christian religious worship."[8]

The *Catechism of the Catholic Church* reiterates this baptismal theology:

> Incorporated into the Church by Baptism, the faithful have received
> the sacramental character that consecrates them for religious worship.
> The baptismal seal enables and commits Christians to serve God by a

---

3. See GIRM, 95.
4. See canon 1247.
5. *Order of Baptism of Children*, 62.
6. LG, 10.
7. LG, 10.
8. LG, 11.

vital participation in the holy liturgy of the Church and to exercise their baptismal priesthood the witness of holy lives and practical charity.[9]

Marked for worship, the faithful are also set apart for service. At confirmation, the baptized receive the fullness of the Holy Spirit. The Spirit comes with spiritual gifts, intending us to use them.

> The gift of the Holy Spirit . . . will be a spiritual seal, by which you will be conformed to Christ and will be made more fully members of his Church. For Christ himself, anointed by the Holy Spirit in the baptism he received from John, was sent forth for the work of his ministry, to pour out on the earth the fire of the same Spirit.[10]

This service takes many forms, as the Holy Spirit's gifts do. We care for the sick; we educate the youth; we bring relief to the traumatized; we advocate for life. The service we offer is not a merely humanitarian effort. It serves the mission of the Church. It proclaims the reign of God. The command of Jesus to love our neighbor motivates us to service. When we act on what we believe with the intention to do God's will, our deeds proclaim to others the Good News of salvation.

All of the baptized are called to work toward the transformation of the world.

—Co-Workers in the
Vineyard of the Lord, p. 8

The baptized proclaim the Gospel in all circumstances: "Reborn as sons and daughters of God, they must profess publicly the faith they have received from God through the church."[11] But they do this in a special way at the Mass. "Both in the offering [sacrifice] and in holy Communion, in their separate ways, though not of course indiscriminately, all have their own part to play in the liturgical action."[12]

Besides participating at Mass, the faithful have other responsibilities as well. They should develop a religious sense, an inner piety. They should show charity toward the brothers and sisters with whom they share the Eucharist.[13] In short, they show on the outside the faith they hold on the inside. Believers also show that faith when they perform some specific responsibility at the liturgy. "The faithful, moreover, should not refuse to serve the People of God in gladness whenever they are asked to perform some particular service or function in the celebration."[14]

---

9. *Catechism of the Catholic Church* (CCC), 1273; quoting LG, 11 and 10.
10. *Order of Confirmation*, 22.
11. LG, 11.
12. LG, 11.
13. See GIRM, 95.
14. GIRM, 97.

Collaborative Ministry

You are most familiar with your own baptismal role when you come to worship. But on the committee it will be good for you to become familiar with as many liturgical ministries as you can. As a member of the liturgy committee, your work will affect their function in the liturgy, and you will need to collaborate with them on a regular basis.

The priest is called the celebrant of the liturgy. The priest "possesses within the Church the sacred power of Orders to offer sacrifice in the person of Christ, presides by this fact over the faithful people gathered here and now, presides over their prayer, proclaims to them the message of salvation, associates the people with himself in the offering of sacrifice through Christ in the Holy Spirit to God the Father, and gives his brothers and sisters the Bread of eternal life and partakes of it with them."[15] He should do this with dignity and humility.

The deacon assists the priest in the orderly celebration of Eucharist. "At Mass, the Deacon has his own part in proclaiming the Gospel, from time to time in preaching God's Word, in announcing the intentions of the universal prayer, in ministering to the Priest, in preparing the altar and in serving the celebration of the Sacrifice, in distributing the Eucharist to the faithful, especially under the species of wine, and from time to time in giving instructions regarding the people's gestures and posture."[16]

Those who assemble as the congregation express their identity as the holy people of God, "a people of God's own possession and a royal Priesthood, so that they may give thanks to God and offer the unblemished sacrificial Victim not only by means of the hands of the Priest but also together with him and so that they may learn to offer their very selves."[17]

> In parishes especially, but also in other Church institutions and communities, lay women and men generously and extensively "cooperate with their pastors in the service of the ecclesial community."*
>
> —Co-Workers in the Vineyard of the Lord, p. 9

Acolytes and servers "serve at the altar and assist the priest and the deacon; these carry the cross, the candles, the thurible, the bread, the wine, and the water, or who are even deputed to distribute Holy Communion as extraordinary ministers."[18]

Readers and lectors proclaim the readings from Scripture, except for the Gospel. They may lead the universal prayer and read the psalm if it is not sung.[19]

---

15. GIRM, 93.
16. GIRM, 94.
17. GIRM, 95.
18. GIRM, 100.
19. See GIRM, 99, 101.
* Paul VI, On *Evangelization in the Modern World* (*Evangelii nuntiandi*), 73, as quoted in the CCC, 910; see also 1 Cor 12:11 and LG, 12.

The choir, the cantor, the psalmist, and instrumentalists all contribute to the singing at Mass. They carry out the parts assigned to them and foster "the active participation of the faithful by means of the singing."[20]

The sacristan "diligently arranges the liturgical books, the vestments, and other things that are necessary for the celebration of Mass."[21]

Other people carry out additional functions: those who greet at the door, those who take up the collection, those who bring forward the gifts, those who offer childcare, and those who set the liturgical environment with the tasteful use of art, flowers, and other items for the delight of the eyes. No one is expert at everything that needs to be done. Instead, the Holy Spirit has dispersed gifts throughout the community. The gathering of these many gifts shows the diversity of the Holy Spirit and the life of the community that has received them in order to share them among the people of God.

Evolvement of the Ministry

There has always been a need to prepare for the liturgy, but the need intensified after the Second Vatican Council. From the earliest days of worship, somebody always had to prepare the Scriptures, the prayers, the bread and wine for the day's celebration. In the centuries following the Council of Trent (1545–1563), the Church further centralized many functions and the liturgy solidified into a predictable pattern. Celebrated in a common language (Latin), following a universal book of texts (*The Roman Missal*), the Mass seemed to be a simple matter to the casual observer. Still, its proper execution demanded the skills of language, posture, and ritual.

The Second Vatican Council (1962–1965) introduced changes to the liturgy for the spiritual welfare of Christians everywhere:

> In order that the Christian people may more surely derive an abundance of graces from the liturgy, the Church desires to undertake with great care a general reform of the liturgy itself. For the liturgy is made up of immutable elements, divinely instituted, and of elements subject to change. These not only may but ought to be changed with the passage of time if they have suffered from the intrusion of anything out of harmony with the inner nature of the liturgy or have become pointless.
>
> In this reform both texts and rites should be so drawn up that they express more clearly the holy things they signify and that the Christian people, as far as possible, are able to understand them with ease and to take part in the rites fully, actively, and as befits a community.[22]

---

20. GIRM, 103; see also GIRM, 102, 104.
21. GIRM, 105a.
22. SC, 21.

The most notable of the changes were in language and posture. The Council permitted the use of vernacular languages in the liturgy, and the priest was allowed to face the people throughout the Mass instead of having his back to them for most of it.

However, there were other extensive changes. The faithful used to participate in silence by following a missal or praying the Rosary. Now they participate through dialogues, song, and action. The lectionary has been expanded tremendously. Previously only 1 percent of the Old Testament and 17 percent of the New Testament were included at the Mass each

For the liturgy is made up of immutable elements, divinely instituted, and of elements subject to change.

—*Sacrosactum concilium*, 21

year. Today, over a three-year cycle, the faithful will hear 14 percent of the Old Testament and 71 percent of the New. Formerly, every Mass used the same Eucharistic Prayer, but now the priest may choose from options. A wider variety of prefaces and other presidential prayers became available.

These changes opened up a new treasury of liturgical music. The Gregorian chant that characterized the earlier liturgy remains a precious gem in the crown of Church music—in the crown of any music in history, for that matter. Now congregations are singing a broader repertoire of music, expressing a fuller range of Catholic beliefs in idioms that resonate with the times and regions of those who sing.

The number of ministers at Mass has grown. Lay ministers have been assigned to some parts of the service, and women have exercised more central roles in the liturgy than in the past—for example, by proclaiming the Scriptures and assisting in the distribution of Communion.

All these changes added new life to the Church's worship. But they came with a price. The liturgy required more preparation. A greater number of people had to be selected, trained, and evaluated. The choice of certain texts had to be made. For this reason, many parishes developed liturgy committees. These were inspired by the Council's call for such committees among Conferences of Bishops and within dioceses. The complexities of the revised liturgy needed more attention, Catholics were enthusiastic about the coming developments, and committees were formed in parishes to help implement the new universal norms.

Over the years since the Council, liturgy committees have undergone some evolution. As people became more familiar with the revisions, they became more practiced at the art of preparing for Mass and other rites. The Vatican continues to release revised liturgical legislation, and the success of these norms requires skilled members of liturgy committees who will discover, read, embrace, and implement them to improve the experience of local worship.

Ritual and Liturgical Law

The liturgy of the Catholic Church is a stylized, ritual prayer. The Church promulgates detailed documents that steer this ritual. The basic format does not change, although significant components do, such as the biblical readings and the Eucharistic Prayer. The solid structure has fluid elements. Still, to a casual observer it may look repetitive and uninteresting. Only those who let the liturgy guide their prayer discover its richness. *Sacrosanctum concilum* states:

> Pastors must therefore realize that when the liturgy is celebrated something more is required than the mere observance of the laws governing valid and lawful celebration; it is also their duty to ensure that the faithful take part fully aware of what they are doing, actively engaged in the rite, and enriched by its effects.[23]

When we perform the prayers and gestures of the liturgy, we repeat what generations of Catholics have done before us.

Each celebration follows a prescribed set of actions and words. These have accumulated and evolved over the long history of the Church. When we perform the prayers and gestures of the liturgy, we repeat what generations of Catholics have done before us. We join with the Church past and present as we anticipate the joyous day of celebration in the future when we will participate fully at the divine liturgy of heaven.

The Church calendar for the liturgical year forms the setting for individual celebrations. The prayer texts for Mass have been carefully composed to draw out the meaning and spirit of seasons and feasts. Wherever you go around the Catholic world, the same prayers and actions are observed in one church after another. This practice stresses the universal nature of our Church, and it forms a global chorus of praise, offering sacrifice and service to God, through Jesus, in the Holy Spirit.

To accomplish this, the Church issues a series of liturgical documents that explain the liturgy and promote its careful celebration. The principal sources of these documents are the Holy See, the conference of bishops, and the diocesan bishop.

The Holy See is also called the Apostolic See. It is the administrative arm of the Roman Catholic Church, and it includes the pope and the various

---

23. SC, 11.

congregations of the curia.[24] In liturgical matters, the pope relies upon the Sacred Congregation for Divine Worship and the Discipline of the Sacraments. As with all congregations, a cardinal is placed in charge of its work. The Apostolic See publishes the liturgical books containing the rites of the Roman Catholic Church. As with all universal communication from the Vatican, the first language of publication is Latin. The Apostolic See reviews and approves the vernacular translations of these texts. The English translations are submitted by the International Commission on English in the Liturgy, a group of bishops representing eleven different conferences, who maintain a common secretariat in Washington, DC. The congregation consults another committee called Vox Clara about translations into English. The Holy See also safeguards the faithful observance of liturgical regulations.[25]

Examples of significant publications from the Holy See include *The Roman Missal*, together with its *General Instruction*, all of the ritual books from the *Rite of Christian Initiation of Adults* to the *Order of Christian Funerals*, as well as the legislation governing vernacular translations, such as *Liturgiam authenticam*.

A conference of bishops is a regional entity, usually formed by the bishops of a particular country. The United States Conference of Catholic Bishops (USCCB) assumes this function in the United States. The primary liturgical responsibility of the conference is the preparation and publication of vernacular translations of the liturgy.[26] The liturgical books authorize the conferences to make some adaptations to the rites, and these adaptations are also included in the respective vernacular translations.[27]

For example, when the third edition of *The Roman Missal* was published in 2011, the USCCB incorporated several adaptations, many of them already being observed, such as a lengthening of the time when the faithful kneel at Mass. These can be found in the *General Instruction of the Roman Missal*.[28] Earlier, the conference omitted the use of the oil of catechumens at the Easter Vigil.[29] It has the authority to make more specific and detailed formularies of the renunciations that precede the profession of faith at baptism, though this has never been done in the United States.[30] The same conference has issued guidelines for art and architecture in Catholic churches.[31] Other more recent changes involve baptism and matrimony. The 2016 *Order of Celebrating Matrimony* (second edition) now includes the optional use of two Hispanic

---

24. See canon 361.
25. Canon 838 §2.
26. See canon 838 §3.
27. See canon 838 §3.
28. See GIRM, 43.
29. See RCIA, 33 §7.
30. See RCIA, 33 §8.
31. See *Built of Living Stones: Art, Architecture, and Worship*.

A bishop may issue liturgical directives for his diocese.

and Filipino traditions: the *arras* and the *lazo*. The 2020 *Order of Baptism of Children* (second edition) clarified a few points, such as the decision that in the United States the use of the anointing with chrism is always included, even in the celebration of baptism of a large number of infants.

The diocesan bishop is the director, promoter, and guardian of the liturgical life in the Church entrusted to him.[32] He may administer policies for the diocese or intervene in singular instances.[33] He may not act contrary to a higher law.[34] The *praenotanda* (foreword or pastoral introduction) of many liturgical books assigns the bishop specific authority concerning some elements of the celebrations. The bishop directs a diocesan commission that promotes the liturgical apostolate.[35]

A bishop may publish diocesan directives concerning the liturgy. For example, he may expand the occasions for Communion under both forms.[36] He may authorize congregations in the United States to remain standing at Mass after the Lamb of God.[37] For a serious reason he may also dispense the elect from participating in one or more of the three scrutinies preceding their initiation.[38]

Liturgical law comes from various sources. Universal legislation is found in the liturgical books, the *Code of Canon Law*, and pronouncements on the liturgy from the Holy See. Some of these statements have more to do with

---

32. See canon 835 §1.
33. Canon 392 §2.
34. See canon 135 §2.
35. See SC, 45.
36. See GIRM, 283.
37. See GIRM, 43.
38. See RCIA, 34 §3.

theology and pastoral care than they do with law. For example, the pope may issue letters or exhortations in this vein, but when he writes an apostolic constitution, he issues a most solemn form of papal legislation. Pope Paul VI's apostolic constitution for the sacrament of confirmation, for example, changed the formula used by a bishop to administer the sacrament. The pope may also issue legislation under the form of *motu proprio*, or "under his own initiative," as Pope Francis did in 2017 when he gave the responsibility of liturgical translations to conferences of bishops.[39]

Dicasteries (departments of the Roman Curia), such as the Sacred Congregation for Divine Worship and the Discipline of the Sacraments, do not issue laws or general decrees unless the pope specifically approves such an action in an individual case.[40] A general decree by the congregation must cite that approval, and it cannot revoke previous legislation.[41] Examples pertaining to the liturgy include *Liturgiam authenticam*, which regulates the translation of Latin liturgical texts into the vernacular languages; *Redemptionis sacramentum*, which addressed a number of liturgical abuses; the *Directory for Masses with Children*, which permits some adjustments at Mass to enhance the way children appreciate the liturgy; and the *Directory for the Application of Principles and Norms on Ecumenism*, which guides the observance of worship between Catholics and other Christians.

Additional norms may be established by the conference of bishops, the diocesan bishop, the vicar general, and the episcopal vicar. A policy established by a diocesan worship office has force only with an express mandate from the bishop or competent vicar. Such law is commonly issued in a statement called a directory. Other documents may be called declarations, norms, or letters.

There is some variation in the weight of these documents, depending on who issues them and why. But all the directives of the Church deserve a charitable and open hearing, as well as a devout intention to carry them out. It is important to note this general norm from *Sacrosanctum concilum*:

> Regulation of the liturgy depends solely on the authority of the Church, that is, on the Apostolic See and, accordingly as the law determines, on the bishop.

> In virtue of power conceded by the law, the regulation of the liturgy within certain defined limits belongs also to various kinds of competent territorial bodies of bishops lawfully established.

---

39. See *Magnum principium*.
40. See *Pastor bonus*, 18.
41. See canon 33 §1.

Therefore, no other person, not even if he is a priest, may on his own add, remove, or change anything in the liturgy.[42]

The Second Vatican Council established guidelines for liturgical adaptation. The faithful around the world received news of this theme with warmth and enthusiasm. Some adaptations are assigned to the conference of bishops. These are generally found in the introductory material to the liturgical books. Others are given to the diocesan bishop. And some are given to the minister. These usually consist of a choice of texts for the sake of the people,[43] or in cases where he is given a sample text and allowed to use "these or similar words."[44] When making these choices, the priest should have the common spiritual good in mind, not his personal preference.

> In arranging the celebration of Mass, the Priest should be attentive rather to the common spiritual good of the People of God than to his own inclinations. He should also remember that choices of this kind are to be made in harmony with those who exercise some part in the celebration, including the faithful, as regards the parts that more directly pertain to them.[45]

More profound adaptations may be made, especially in mission territories, with the approval of the Apostolic See.

Sometimes a norm is established through custom rather than law. In this case, the longstanding custom of a particular community becomes its norm. Customs may obtain the force of law after thirty years of continuous observance.[46]

Some adaptations to the liturgy may and should happen. Ordinarily, however, it is best to know the universal and local liturgical laws, and to let them guide the work of a liturgy committee. The two books you will want to know the best are *The Roman Missal* and the *Lectionary for Mass*.

The rules and regulations for liturgy are meant to ensure its smooth execution. They hope to deepen the community's experience of prayer. Some people are put off by liturgical law on the grounds that it stifles the Spirit, but it is meant to enliven the Spirit on a different level. You never grow tired of your favorite music. You get something more out of a favorite book every time you read it. You return to a certain body of water, a spectacular view, or a special building time and again because it renews you every

> **Even in the liturgy the Church does not wish to impose a rigid uniformity in matters which do not affect the faith or the good of the whole community; rather, the Church respects and fosters the genius and talents of the various races and peoples.**
>
> —*Sacrosanctum concilium*, 37

---

42. SC, 22.
43. See GIRM, 24 and 352.
44. You will notice this phrasing throughout the ritual books of the Church.
45. See GIRM, 352.
46. See canons 23–28.

time you experience it. The same is true for liturgical prayer. The more we enter it, the more it speaks to us.

Good liturgy is any liturgy in which people use their God-given gifts. They praise God as best as they are able. You do not have to have the most skilled musicians or the most expressive reader. You do not need the best homilist or the strongest congregational singing. It matters that everyone comes ready to render thanks to God, using the gifts of the Spirit with the measure in which they are bestowed. Too many people evaluate liturgy based on what they got out of it. That is not the point. The point is what *God* gets out of it. God deserves our full attention, the abandonment of our other concerns, and the devotion of our thoughts and deeds to him.

Questions for Discussion and Reflection

1. What place does the liturgy have in your life? Do your weekend plans revolve around the liturgy or do you fit the liturgy in when you can? Has this changed as you have grown in faith?

2. Why is taking part in the liturgy important to you? What are your first remembrances of participating at Mass? When did attending Mass change from something you do out of obligation to something that you look forward to?

3. Think about a time when the liturgy has touched you. What sounds, smells, words, and images do you recall? How did these affect you at the time? How did they affect you later?

4. Consider a time when the liturgy influenced you to mend a relationship. Reflect on how gestures, actions, and words in the liturgy softened your heart.

5. What areas of the Church's liturgical law do you wish you knew better? What steps can you take to learn more?

Chapter Three

Serving on the Liturgy Committee

*Given the nature of Sunday Mass and its importance in the lives
of the faithful, it must be prepared with special care.*

— *Dies Domini*, 50

You are serving your community as a member of the liturgy committee.
Your work is essential for the smooth execution of the complicated liturgies of the Roman Catholic Church. You will bring experience, energy, and
ideas to your work. You will also bring a willing spirit that desires to do what
is best for those with whom you worship.

The Work of the Liturgy Committee

When you serve on a liturgy committee, you can more dramatically catch the
vision of the entire liturgical year, the expanse of liturgical celebrations in
the Church's repertoire of prayer and devotional life, and the details of the
rites that accent the journey of individual Catholics from their initiation through
their moments of passage and on to their final rest. At the most and least significant times in the lives of individuals and communities, the Church is there.
We bring centuries of experience to our rituals. We help people drink from the
deep waters of our tradition.

Because of the nature of Catholic worship, it may be better to think of your
role as preparing the liturgy, rather than planning it.[1] You don't plan for Mass
the way you plan a meal, deciding what food to use and how to prepare it.
Rather, you prepare the Mass the way you prepare food from a good recipe.
You know the formula, but now you make it. You use the guidelines together
with your own creativity, spirit, and experience.

Even so, preparing is only one step. People will celebrate the liturgy you
helped prepare, and then they will think about it. Members of the liturgy committee will evaluate the ministers, the music, and the success of their preparations for individual days and entire liturgical seasons. With these insights,
they will make better preparations in the future.

The liturgy committee also does more than prepare and evaluate the liturgies in the parish. The committee prays well together and assists the community in its public prayer. It sets goals, direction, and principles for the
liturgical life of the community. The committee functions as a sounding board
for the parishioners and is comfortable with asking and taking on challenging

---

1. See Austin H. Fleming and Victoria M. Tufano, *Preparing for Liturgy: A Theology and Spirituality*
(Chicago: Liturgy Training Publications, 1997).

The liturgy committee is visionary.

questions and issues. The committee works hard at celebrating well—it provides a basis for what they need and values the liturgy as the most important work of the parish community.

A brief job description of a parish liturgy committee includes the following:

- puts primary attention on doing the basics especially well, Sunday after Sunday—the essential actions of gathering, welcoming, proclaiming, and reflecting on the Word of God, and celebrating Eucharist;

- assesses and evaluates the needs of the worshipping assembly;

- advises and provides direction for those who prepare liturgies, including the parish liturgist, musicians, and presiding ministers;

- offers liturgical catechesis, for the liturgy and from the liturgy, to all parishioners;

- promotes the development of competent liturgical ministers and works to create guidelines and patterns for all liturgical ministers; sacramental, devotional, and domestic Church celebrations; weekday Masses; special feasts; and holydays of obligation;

- sets goals for the progress of the liturgical, sacramental, and devotional life of the parish;

- implements directives from the universal Church, the diocesan Church, and the local parish;

- maintains ongoing communication with the pastoral council, other parish committees, and organizations (such as the social justice committee, sacramental staff, and religious education).

There is often a tension between the "nuts and bolts" of preparing particular liturgies and providing liturgical formation. For example, does the liturgy committee simply decide who's going to buy flowers—and what kind of flowers—or does the committee deal with deeper concepts and issues? Here we follow a simple principle: *leave these and other decisions to the experts.* Who are the *experts?* They will be different people in every community. They could be paid or volunteer, full time or part time, and they could serve as pastoral associate, director of liturgy, director of liturgy and music, or just director of music. The experts can also be a group of talented individuals who form subcommittees of the liturgy committee to prepare the music, the environment, and the various rites.

Because liturgy is at the heart of parish life, the liturgy committee and its work need to be among the highest priorities. The parish liturgy committee should understand that its primary responsibility is not necessarily to prepare the details for liturgical celebrations. The committee's primary role is *setting a vision* for the celebration of the liturgy in the community and providing liturgical formation for its members and the entire parish. Since liturgy is a work of art, it should be prepared by artists. Whether it is a small group of experts or members of the parish liturgy committee who are charged with the task of preparing and evaluating the liturgy, everyone involved in the process must know, love, and respect the members of the liturgical assembly.

The liturgy committee may set goals for the sacramental life of the parish.

The liturgy committee may also spend time working together with other staff members to develop guidelines for the celebration of the sacraments. It is important to have clear liturgical guidelines that respect the rites and are at the same time pastoral and flexible. When guidelines are in place, the parish can provide the appropriate tools for those who are preparing for the sacraments and those who may need to have the celebration of the sacraments delayed. Formulation of liturgical guidelines for the parish celebration of the sacraments—especially regarding funerals, weddings, infant baptism, and Christian initiation for children, youth, and adults—are the first to formulate if no guidelines are yet in place.

Membership

Who makes up the liturgy committee is going to depend on the size of your parish and who is on staff. Perhaps yours is a community that has both a salaried liturgy director and a salaried music director. If so, both should be part of a liturgy committee. In some instances, these roles are assumed by the same individual. At the same time, there are parishes who do not have salaried liturgy personnel. Even in those situations, someone somehow is coordinating liturgy. This could be a volunteer or perhaps a deacon or associate pastor designated by the pastor. Whoever is directing needs to be present.

Besides those who direct liturgy and/or music, who else should be in attendance? Since the presider is a critical component of every liturgical celebration, either the pastor or his representative needs to be part of the group. In addition, there should be a representative from the various liturgical ministries such as the lectors and readers, extraordinary ministers of holy Communion, hospitality ministers, those who prepare the liturgical environment, and so on. One or two members-at-large can also be a welcome addition, acting as representatives of the assembly, the most important ministry at liturgy.

If they are agreeable to doing so, the coordinator for the sacraments of initiation (both for adults and children) and possibly the director of faith formation might also attend as needed. When details of the Triduum are going to be discussed, inviting the director of sacramental formation to provide input makes sense. Or perhaps you would like to see more youth serve as liturgical ministers. Invite the director of faith formation or the youth minister, if you have one, to consider how that can be accomplished. Building bridges with parish staff members and other committees fosters a cooperative spirit that will enhance the entire faith community.

The liturgy committee will want to be in regular dialogue with other parish committees, especially the pastoral council, social justice committee, and sacramental preparation committee. It is essential to keep lines of communication open with these groups so the parish council and parish staff will not be faced with any surprises, and so they can have an opportunity to take part in the decision-making process for any changes that may be implemented into the liturgical life of the parish.[2]

> Together with the ordained ministry, other ministries, whether formally instituted or simply recognized, can flourish for the good of the whole community, sustaining it in all its many needs: from catechesis to liturgy, from the education of the young to the widest array of charitable works.
>
> — *Novo millennio ineunte*, 46

---

2. LTPs *Sourcebook for Sundays, Seasons, and Weekdays* provides a supplemental resource for worship committees to use when discussing sacramental rites and beyond. It's accessible as a free download on the product page www.LTP.org/SSS.

Most importantly, a liturgy committee functions best when it reflects the makeup of the parish. Thus, the group should consist of men and women of varying ages and cultures and possibly even a youth representative. The members of the committee, therefore, should be an eclectic representation of the parish, be registered parishioners, and model full, conscious, and active participation in the liturgical and sacramental life of the community.

Qualities of a Committee Member

Those who serve on a liturgy committee should be practicing Catholics who fully participate in Mass on a regular basis. They should have a passion for the liturgy and its ability to transform lives. They need a rudimentary knowledge of liturgy, such as the structure of the Mass and its flow, some basic knowledge of the liturgy documents, an understanding of the various liturgical roles, and a respect for liturgy as a ritual celebration governed by liturgical law. Some individuals may come lacking some of this knowledge, but still qualify if they have a desire to learn.

Knowledge of the community is a critical piece for those who would serve on a liturgy committee. What are the demographics of the parish? What is the parish's history and its legitimate traditions that are in harmony with the values of the Second Vatican Council? Members who are newer to the community will need to pair up with someone who can provide them with this information.

Ministry in the Church continues the ministry of Jesus through the ages and throughout the world. Continually, the Spirit calls forth new ministries and new ministers to serve evolving needs, as the history of the Church shows.

—*Co-Workers in the Vineyard of the Lord*, p. 26

Liturgy committee members are people who were recognized for their leadership skills and invited to serve. They have good communication skills, especially the ability to listen to others. They work well with others and can motivate them as well. They treat others and their opinions with the same respect and dignity they expect for themselves. Above all, they know that unity does not equate with uniformity. They value the diversity that exists in every parish community.

Because the only constant is change, these people possess flexibility, a sense of humor, an ability to collaborate with others, and a genuine love for the community they serve. All that they do is informed by their personal prayer life. Not every member will possess every quality to the same degree. All will have different strengths and learn from each other as well.

Members of the liturgy committee may select designated leaders (chairperson and vice-chairperson) as well as a person to record the minutes of the meeting (secretary). A discernment process should take place at a meeting early in the year to decide who the chairperson and secretary for the committee will be. This service could be for three years and may be renewed for an additional three years. However, it is important for others to step up and assume leadership as well. Rotating one or two new people into the committee each year will be important for keeping the focus of the group fresh and alive with new insights and observations.

Formation

Whether you sign up to volunteer at an animal shelter or the local food pantry, some kind of preliminary training is required. Likewise, those who serve on a parish liturgy committee need formation to carry out the tasks of a liturgy committee and accomplish the goals the group has established. This means every member needs basic knowledge in the following areas:

- The structure of the liturgy / parts of the Mass
- The liturgical year / the seasons
- The role of music in the liturgy
- The role of environment and art
- The difference between devotional prayer and liturgical prayer

The committee's formation should begin with the primary sources *Sacrosanctum concilium* and the *General Instruction of the Roman Missal*. A good facilitator can lead the group through these documents with some well thought out questions to get everyone thinking about their role and how liturgy is being done in their parish community. New members will also benefit from an evening of orientation overviewing the history of the committee, how the group operates, and its recent accomplishments.

Once a group is up and running, its members will want to advance their understanding of liturgy. This can be accomplished in several ways. Select a book for the year and read a section each month. One of the following titles could be a good starting place: *Liturgy with Style and Grace: Third Edition, Revised* by Gabe Huck; *The Liturgy: The Source and Summit of Our Christian Life* by Corinna Laughlin, or *Guide for Celebrating Sunday Mass* by Paul Turner. The books by Huck and Laughlin have discussion questions at the end of each chapter to facilitate discussion.

Catechesis both precedes the Liturgy and springs from it.

—*National Directory for Catechesis*, 33

Subscribing to a worthy periodical can also be a source of education for the group. *Pastoral Liturgy*® magazine meets this requirement. A subscription for each member will give the group more than enough material to learn from and discuss throughout the year. Likewise, Catholic publishers offer annual preparation resources that guide the committee throughout the year, such as *Sourcebook for Sundays, Seasons, and Weekdays: The Almanac for Pastoral Liturgy*.[3]

---

3. All of the resources mentioned above are published by Liturgy Training Publications (www.LTP.org).

If your diocesan office issues a new directive, the liturgy committee will need to study it themselves before sharing the information with the appropriate ministers and the entire community if needed. Becoming familiar with any revised liturgical books would be time well spent by the group. One could spend a year on the new translation of the *Order of Baptism of Children* (or another ritual book), studying, observing current practices, making recommendations, and then overseeing implementation. Invite those involved with these rituals to attend the committee meetings. Who better than the coordinator of Christian initiation to educate the commission on the process? Who better than one of your deacons to introduce the group to the Liturgy of the Hours (or your pastor or another staff person if a member of a religious community)? What about the music director to explore the role of music in the liturgy?

It is desirable that members of the committee attend liturgies outside of the parish. A good place to start is at the other parishes in the same deanery or vicariate. A visit to the diocesan cathedral at least once a year is a must for all members of the liturgy committee. When visiting other parishes, return with the parish bulletin or any other publications

Engage adults actively in the actual life and ministry of the Christian community.

—*Our Hearts Were Burning within Us*, 83

that will benefit your community. Bring a camera. Taking pictures of various worship spaces and decor will be helpful to the work of the committee.

Finally, the group should be led with an assessment of their formation. Where do they feel most knowledgeable? Where do they need more training? What would they like to learn more about? Answering these questions will help you determine your next steps.

At some point, you may have a situation where only one or two members need initial formation. Perhaps you can team up with one or two neighboring parishes to provide initial training for their members and yours as well. This would be a good use of everyone's time and resources. If that is not possible, you could pair up the new member with a seasoned member. They could meet outside of the regular meeting time and review some of the basic liturgy documents, much like an initiation sponsor or candidate relationship.

Always check with your diocesan liturgy office to see what workshops they are offering that might be appropriate for a new member. Publishing companies such as Liturgy Training Publications and Ave Maria Press are two that offer virtual workshops at little or no cost. And, if it has been a while since the group received initial training, they might profit from a refresher course along with the new recruits.

Forming the Assembly

A liturgy committee exists to help the faithful have an experience of good liturgy when they gather to pray. When celebrations are done well, the faithful learn over time what good liturgy looks like. If they are poorly celebrated, that too will educate the people in the pew but in a less than favorable manner. Good liturgy is a form of evangelization and is the primary way that people learn what it means to be in relationship with God and with each other. As the *Directory for Masses with Children* states, "[T]he liturgy itself always exerts its own inherent power to instruct."[4]

Aside from this important fact, it is the responsibility of the liturgy committee to keep the assembly well informed about upcoming liturgical events. Even if you think "they should know that by now," you probably need to offer a gentle nudge. The seasoned parishioner needs reminders, and for sure, the newcomer will appreciate knowing how the community does reposition of the Blessed Sacrament on Holy Thursday. Also, it has been said that people need to hear something seven times before they make it their own.

Bulletin articles can be helpful though not everyone reads them. Brief presentations at Mass or something simple in the announcements are other avenues. If, for instance, you are making a significant change in your communion procession, you may want to include a short demonstration before Mass for the visual learner.[5]

If your parish has a website or a Facebook account, these, too, can be avenues for learning. Posting short videos on the parish website or social media pages and electronic communications such as Flocknotes may be paths to explore. Because parishes are so diverse, we need to address that reality with as many formational opportunities as possible.[6]

Evangelization with joy becomes beauty in the liturgy, as part of our daily concern to spread goodness. The Church evangelizes and is herself evangelized through the beauty of the liturgy, which is both a celebration of the task of evangelization and the source of her renewed self-giving.

—*Evangelii gaudium*, 24

Formation of Liturgical Ministers

In fairness to the liturgical minister, and out of respect for the liturgy, those who serve in a liturgical ministry need to be properly prepared for their role. In a broad sense, this, too, is a task of the liturgy committee—that is, they are responsible to see that it is taking place and being done well.

How this happens will depend on your situation. If you have a salaried liturgy director, she or he will probably do much of the training, though not

---

4. *Directory for Masses with Children*, 12.
5. Liturgy Training Publications provides bulletin insert resources such as *Keeping the Seasons: Bilingual Print and Digital Resources for Your Parish* (available for Advent and Christmas Time and Lent, Triduum, and Easter Time) and *Bulletin Inserts for the Life of the Parish* (separate volumes on devotions and customs, liturgical ministers, the liturgical year, and more).
6. Liturgy Training Publications offers many short videos that can be used for catechesis. They are often posted on their Facebook (https://www.facebook.com/LiturgyTrainingPublications/) and Instagram pages (liturgytrainingpublications).

Every meeting should incorporate time for prayer and ongoing formation.

necessarily alone. If training lectors, the liturgy director could handle the theological aspects of the ministry with the lector chairperson explaining the nuts and bolts of the ministry.

Some dioceses hold ministry training workshops. Some are for the ministers themselves, while others train the trainer, who then brings that information back to the parish community.

Developing job descriptions and simple handbooks for servers, hospitality ministers, lectors and readers, and extraordinary ministers of holy Communion could be a yearlong project for a committee. Such documents would then be included in the initial training for those ministers.

Ongoing training should be an expectation for all. At least once a year it is helpful to bring the lectors together to collectively look at their ministry and how they are doing. This kind of evening could be led by an outside speaker or someone within the community. Your budget and resources will determine where you turn.[7]

The Meeting Agenda

Having an agenda enables a group to accomplish its goals. In addition, agendas help a group pay attention to the tasks outlined in its job description. For example, evaluating the liturgical seasons is an ongoing task of a liturgy committee. To get this accomplished, evaluations need to be slotted at the

---

7.   The United States Conference of Catholic Bishops provides this pastoral article regarding ways parishes can implement liturgical catechesis: https://www.usccb.org/beliefs-and-teachings/how-we-teach/catechesis /catechetical-sunday/word-of-god/upload/catechesis-and-liturgy-pdf-03-40-22.pdf.

appropriate meeting: Advent and Christmas in January, Lent and the Triduum soon after Easter, and so on.

Most parish committees are required to turn in their budgets in the early spring. If that is the case, a liturgy committee will need to work on its budget in February or March at the latest. In addition, a committee may have set one or two goals that need to be addressed during the year. Perhaps you decided to host a Morning of Renewal for all your liturgical ministers. This goal will then appear on more than one agenda as you work out the details of a speaker, the logistics of the day, refreshments, and so on.

Prepare a detailed agenda and keep to the time frame.

And then there is the unexpected. A new diocesan directive may need the group's attention. Or another group within the parish may need your help. These items will need to be slotted so they are discussed and not forgotten.

While tasks and goals are important agenda items, there are other components as well. Every meeting needs to include prayer and some ongoing formation.[8] In addition, those who serve on the committee will want to have an opportunity to communicate regarding their particular areas of worship. They may also wish to seek the committee's wisdom if they are grappling with an issue.

Ministry reports are fine but are best submitted with the agenda. All can read them ahead of the meeting time and seek clarification as needed. It is possible to utilize part of the meeting for reports as long as they don't take over.

At least one week prior to the board's meeting, an agenda should be sent to each member, clearly outlining the order of business. This agenda can be sent out by the chairperson of the liturgy committee after conferring with the person responsible for directing liturgy in the parish. If there are articles or other documents that need to be read in advance, be sure to include them with the agenda. Such preparation ensures that the members come well prepared and spend their time profitably. No one wants to waste their time or revisit the same agenda item month after month.[9]

Frequency and Length of the Meetings

Although most parish committees meet monthly, you need not feel compelled to do so. Taking a break is okay. In fact, you may want to do so intentionally,

---

8. See page 30.
9. LTP's *Sourcebook for Sundays, Seasons, and Weekdays* includes seasonal agendas.

eliminating a December meeting when all are preoccupied with family celebrations and such. Some avoid meeting in July as well. Consider utilizing one of those months for a social gathering. Those who play and pray together will work better together. The determining factor for when to schedule meetings is to make sure you are preparing for a particular season or observance well in advance. Here are some examples for when the liturgy committee should be meeting:

Season or Feast	Initial Preparation	Final Preparation	Evaluation
Advent	mid-September	mid-October	following the season
Christmas (Vigil through Day)	mid-September	mid-October	following the season
Christmas Time (Holy Family— Baptism of the Lord)	early October	early November	following the season
Ordinary Time during Winter	mid-November	mid-December	following the season
Lent	late December	mid-January	following the season
Sacred Paschal Triduum	early January	early February	following the season
Easter Time	late January	late February	following the season
Ordinary Time (weeks 9 to 15)	late March	late April	following the weeks
Ordinary Time (weeks 16 to 26)	late May	late June	following the weeks
Ordinary Time (weeks 27 to 34)	late July	late August	following the weeks
Patronal Feast or Anniversary	Three months before	Two months before	Two weeks after liturgy
Special Observance (i.e. Confirmation, etc.)	Three months before	Two months before	Two weeks after liturgy

This table was adapted from Groundwork: Planning Liturgical Seasons by Yvonne Cassa and Joanne Sanders © 1988, Liturgy Training Publications, Archdiocese of Chicago.

As a general rule, an hour to an hour and a half or two hours should be enough time to cover most issues. Talk this over at a meeting to see if all are comfortable with such parameters. Once in place, do respect the time of the volunteers. Consistently running over time can quickly become a source of annoyance. You can also save time by avoiding discussions that should take place elsewhere, such as in a subcommittee. Not everyone needs to discuss the details of every agenda item.

A successful meeting requires the skills of an excellent facilitator, one who will make sure everyone's opinion is heard and considered, while keeping the group on task. Most of the time the facilitator will be the chairperson of the liturgy committee unless you decide to rotate this responsibility.

Just as important as an agenda are the minutes from a meeting. They need not be lengthy, but they should clearly summarize what was discussed. If there are actions that need to be addressed before the next meeting, let them be reflected in the minutes. This means the minutes should go out to the membership in a timely manner in order to be helpful.

Another consideration might be a timekeeper. To avoid spending too much time on one topic and running out of time, agree at the beginning of the meeting how much time should be devoted to each agenda item. Then stick to it! If need be, something might have to be postponed to another meeting.

Prayer

Prayer is a nonnegotiable component of every liturgy committee meeting. In fact, it is difficult to imagine beginning such a liturgy committee meeting any other way since its focus is the communal prayer life of the parish. Leaders of the parish liturgy committee should ask for volunteers from the committee to lead prayer from meeting to meeting. Not everyone will be comfortable leading in front of others. Be sure to give those time to prepare, and try to avoid putting people on the spot to lead spontaneously and at the last minute.

So how shall we pray? There are two ritual books that will come in handy for praying at liturgy committee meetings. First, there is the *Book of Blessings*. The *Book of Blessings* includes orders of blessings for various circumstances: families, the needs of people, the liturgical year, places, and things. In chapter 6 you will find blessings of those gathered at a meeting, including the beautiful prayer that was used before every session at the Second Vatican Council.[10] You can simply say the prayer together. Or take it a step further and "break it open" with one or two simple questions: What word or phrase is speaking to you in this prayer, right now? How is this prayer speaking to our work as a liturgy committee?

---

10. This prayer has been provided for you in this resource on page 72.

You might also consult *Catholic Household Blessings and Prayers*, which is published by the United States of Conference of Catholic Bishops. This resource is very similar to the *Book of Blessings*, but it has been adapted for home ritual purposes. In chapter 5, you will find prayers for Catholic living. These prayers may be suitable to begin your meetings.[11]

Liturgy Training Publications also publishes an annual resource of prayer, *Daily Prayer*. It is loosely based on the Liturgy of the Hours and may be used to pray anytime during the day and throughout the year. Each member of the committee may be given a copy of this book and may rotate responsibilities using it to begin prayer.

Since liturgy committees are about the business of parish worship, reflecting on the Gospel or the psalm for the coming Sunday is an excellent way to pray. The one who is leading prayer can have one or two simple questions that invite faith sharing in a nonthreatening manner.

You can also "break open" one of the Eucharistic Prayers or have a fruitful discussion on the lyrics of a hymn you are currently using. Imagine pondering these words from "As We Gather at Your Table":

> Turn our worship into witness
> In the sacrament of life;
> Send us forth to love and serve you,
> Bringing peace where there is strife.
>
> Give us, Christ, your great compassion
> To forgive as you forgave;
> May we still behold your image
> In the world you died to save.[12]

While beginning your meeting with prayer sets the tone, you can also send everyone off with a brief prayer perhaps inviting everyone who wishes to verbalize a petition they wish the group to prayer for. Incorporating prayer into every meeting is not just a nice thing to do. It is a way that each member has an opportunity to deepen their faith one prayer at a time.

A Scripture reading or reflection is not a prayer in and of itself but may be part of a larger order of prayer. For example, begin and end with the sign of the cross or the Glory Be. Invite people to pause for a moment of silence and then introduce the Word of God or a chosen reflect. Time for shared reflection may follow. Close with a prayer that is similar in structure to the collect at Mass. "A simple way to construct this prayer is to use this format, **You, Who, Do, Through**. Address the prayer to God, the Father (**You**) and note that he

---

11. Liturgy Training Publications also publishes *Catholic Meeting Prayers*, which includes forty-seven prayer services designed to address the most common needs of the liturgical year. This book requires little to no preparation, allowing any staff member, volunteer, or committee to lead your group in prayer.
12. "As We Gather At Your Table"; words: Carl P. Daw Jr.; © 1989 Hope Publishing Company, Carol Stream, IL 60188. All rights reserved. Used by permission.

acts in a particular way (**Who**). Indicate something the Father or Son has done or will do for us (**Do**) and conclude with the doxological ending (**Through**)."[13] "By an ancient tradition of the Church, the Collect prayer is usually addressed to God the Father, through Christ, in the Holy Spirit, and is concluded with a Trinitarian ending."[14] However, the prayers may also be addressed to Christ (you will find such prayers in the ritual texts of the Church). Collect prayers aren't addressed to the Holy Spirit. The response is of course, "Amen," which means "so-be-it" or "I believe."

> **You:** Lord of all,
> **Who:** you call us to listen to your Word
> and help us to ponder the paschal mystery of Christ.
> **Do:** Keep us mindful that Christ's life, death, and
> is celebrated daily within each of
> our lives and transforms our hearts.
> **Through:** Through Christ our Lord.[15]

The doxological ending will depend upon how you addressed the prayer. As noted in the *General Instruction*,[16]

- "If the prayer is directed to the Father: Through our Lord Jesus Christ, your Son, who lives and reigns with you in the unity of the Holy Spirit, God, for ever and ever;[17]

- "If it is directed to the Father, but the Son is mentioned at the end: Who lives and reigns with you in the unity of the Holy Spirit, God, for ever and ever;[18]

- "If it is directed to the Son: Who live and reign with God the Father in the unity of the Holy Spirit, God, for ever and ever."[19]

Even at meetings, the person leading prayer should take their cue from the liturgy. Create a prayerful environment in the room, such as dimmer lights and a lighted candle. Use a ritual book or ritual binder rather than sheets of paper. If music is included prepare a worship aid for the committee members to use. Invite committee members to proclaim the reading or reflection. Those who are proclaiming and leading prayer should stand.

Who should lead prayer at the meetings? It need not always be the pastor or the deacon. The role of prayer leader can be rotated, providing that everyone

---

13. Corinna Laughlin, *United in Christ: Preparing the Liturgy of the Word at Catholic Weddings* (Chicago: Liturgy Training Publications, 2016), 87.

14. GIRM, 54.

15. Mary Heinrich, *Daily Prayer 2021* (Chicago: Liturgy Training Publications, 2020), 256.

16. GIRM, 56.

17. The shorter form of this doxology is "Through Christ our Lord."

18. The shorter form of this doxology is "Who lives and reigns for ever and ever."

19. The shorter form of this doxology is "Who live and reign for ever and ever."

The liturgy committee should take time to evaluate past liturgies and sacramental rites.

is comfortable in that position. No one should ever be forced to contribute during faith sharing or take on a role for which they do not feel ready.

Finally, if possible, have your group pray together outside of the usual meeting time. Once or twice a year, could you participate in the same weekend liturgy? Sit together and go out for coffee afterward? Could you go together to Stations of the Cross? Pray together during exposition of the Blessed Sacrament? Join other parish groups to pray Evening Prayer? These experiences will build your team and also inspire your parish community when they see you together in this way. The team that prayers together works best together.

Evaluation

Time should be set aside for the liturgy committee to evaluate the parish's liturgical, sacramental, and devotional life. The philosopher Socrates said: "The unexamined life is not worth living." Over two thousand years later, this quotation gives us a sound reason for evaluating our progress, our successes, and our failures.

If we stop and think about it, evaluations are going on all the time. Consider those casual conversations that go on among members outside the meeting room discussing the pros and cons of last week's music selections. Some of those discussions might bear fruit, but what is really called for is a deliberate, intentional examination of what we are doing and how we are doing it. Without such discussions we are not likely to achieve our goals and fulfill our main objective as a liturgy committee—a good and prayerful experience of liturgy for the community.

Let's say your liturgy committee has determined that the way in which the Communion Rite is celebrated needs some attention. The entire group observed the rite over a period and brought their observations to a liturgy meeting. From your discussion, you decided to make three changes that involve communicating with the extraordinary ministers of holy Communion, the priests and deacons, hospitality ministers, and the assembly. Now, three months have gone by. Do you just move on? Not yet—not until you have taken the time to evaluate what is going well and what might still need improvement. Taking the time for this important step will allow you to feel good about what you have accomplished as a group. At the same time, it will open your eyes to what might be the next task for your group.

Besides evaluating the goals you have set for yourselves, think about evaluating your meetings, especially if you find yourself getting buried in the same discussions month after month. Evaluating the various liturgical seasons is also time well spent. Certainly, each liturgical ministry could evaluate how they are doing, and you will surely want to do a general kind of parish liturgical evaluation that can help the group prioritize where they need to focus in the coming year or years. This form is provided as a supplement on the LTP website.[20]

If you still think evaluations aren't all that necessary, think again. An honest evaluation is a tool that keeps us focused on our goals and how well we are achieving them. Down the line, evaluations can also provide new members with a concrete history of what the group has worked on and how well it went.

Encouragement for Your Ministry

All of the writers who contributed to this book work in parishes with liturgy committees like yours. Like you, we find our ministry to be richly rewarding and at times a source of frustration. The very fact that you have this book in hand indicates that you take seriously the work of providing good liturgy. You care about your parish community and their commu-

> Be filled with the Spirit, addressing one another in psalms and hymns and spiritual songs, singing and playing to the Lord in your hearts.
>
> —Ephesians 5:18b–19

nal prayer. You are aware that you have been entrusted with a responsibility that requires time, effort, and patience. Yet despite the challenges, you persevere, dedicated to upholding the vision of the Second Vatican Council. We are certain that "the one who began a good work in you will continue to complete it until the day of Christ Jesus."[21] May "your love may increase ever more and more in knowledge and every kind of perception."[22]

---

20. See https://www.ltp.org/products/details/ELMLC2/guide-for-liturgy-committees-second-edition.
21. Philippians 1:6.
22. Philippians 1:9.

Questions for Discussion and Reflection

1. Considering that, as a member of the liturgy committee, you are expected to be an ambassador of the liturgy to the people of your parish, helping to promote catechesis about the liturgy and carrying the people's concerns and questions to the liturgy committee, how comfortable are you as a communicator and mediator? If you do not have much experience or comfort in that role, what would help you to grow into it?

2. Realizing that your group will help guide many decisions about the liturgy, how well do you understand and feel inspired by the vision of the liturgy given to us by the Second Vatican Council? What are some ways you might learn more about that vision? When have you experienced liturgy imbued with that spirit? What effects of it did you observe in yourself and others?

3. Because the liturgy always sends the people out on mission to "announce the Gospel of the Lord" and to glorify the Lord by their lives, how well do you understand the ways that the liturgy instructs and inspires people to do that? How clearly do you see the link between liturgy and justice? How could you become more aware and help others see it?

Chapter Four

Spirituality and Discipleship

So when [Jesus] had washed [the disciples'] feet [and] put his
garments back on and reclined at table again, he said to them,
"Do you realize what I have done for you?"

—John 13:12

U nlike the other evangelists, John does not describe the meal itself in his
account of the Last Supper. Instead, he concentrates on what happens
after supper when Jesus kneels to wash the feet of his disciples. This action on
the part of Jesus unfolds in silence until Jesus comes to Peter, who strenuously
objects. The name by which Peter addresses Jesus—"Master"[1]—says it all: how
can Jesus, the Master, take on the task of a slave? In reply, Jesus gently tells
Peter that now is not the time for explanation—all will become clear later on.
But when Peter stubbornly insists, "You will never wash my feet,"[2] Jesus
explains. Everything depends on this: if Jesus does not wash Peter's feet, Peter
will have "no inheritance"[3] with him. After he has finished washing their feet,
Jesus asks them all: *Do you realize what I have done for you?*[4]

The experience of the disciples is often our
experience in the liturgy, because in the liturgy
Jesus is still kneeling down to wash the feet of his
disciples. He shares his divine wisdom with us,
holding nothing back. He serves us, feeding us with

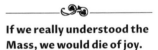

**If we really understood the
Mass, we would die of joy.**

—St. John Vianney

own his Body and Blood. And he still asks us that question, "Do you realize
what I have done for you?"[5] Knowing how to celebrate the liturgy is important.
But that is only the beginning. When Jesus asks this question of his disciples,
he is not asking them for a theological explanation of the ritual action he has
just carried out. He is asking something deeper. He is asking about their relationship with him. "Do you realize what I have done for you?"[6]

As members of the liturgy committee, we spend a good amount of time
learning the liturgy—and there is much to learn! Knowing the seasons and
feasts of the liturgical year, understanding the development and flow of the
Eucharistic liturgy, and being familiar with the rubrics of the Church are all
important for those entrusted with the planning and preparation of parish

---

1. John 13:13.
2. John 13:8.
3. John 13:8.
4. John 13:12.
5. John 13:12.
6. John 13:12.

36

liturgy. But the question Jesus asks the disciples is ultimately the most important one. Because in the liturgy, something *happens*. Jesus is present and invites us into relationship with him, not only as individuals but as a community of believers. When we realize what Jesus does for us in the liturgy, we will be better able to help others enter more fully into the Mass and experience its fruits.

Service and Spirituality

When we serve in a liturgical ministry, it is not just one more hobby to add interest to our lives. Liturgical ministry is unique because it becomes part of our worship, part of our faith life. We need to recognize Christ in and through our ministry, or we will go stale pretty quickly! Our faith should inform our service on the liturgy committee, and vice versa: our service on the liturgy committee, carried out in a spirit of discipleship, can help lead us to genuine service of others.

When it comes to lay people carrying out ministries in the liturgy, *Sacrosanctum concilium* has this to say:

> In liturgical celebrations each one, minister or layperson, who has an office to perform, should do all of, but only, those parts which pertain to that office.[7]

> Servers, readers, commentators, and members of the choir also exercise a genuine liturgical function. They ought to discharge their office, therefore, with the sincere devotion and decorum demanded by so exalted a ministry and rightly expected of them by God's people.[8]

> Consequently, they must all be deeply imbued with the spirit of the liturgy, in the measure proper to each one, and they must be trained to perform their functions in a correct and orderly manner.[9]

A lot is expected of liturgical ministers! They need to know what they are called to do—and what they are *not* called to do. They need to carry out their ministry with deep reverence and dignity because what they do is important, and because the community they serve is important. They need to know what they are doing and they need to do it right. And through all this, they need to be "deeply imbued with the spirit of the liturgy." It is a fascinating phrase. What does it mean to be imbued with the spirit of the liturgy? What exactly *is* the spirit of the liturgy?

There are many ways to answer that question because the liturgy is our source and our summit, an inexhaustible source of grace. In this chapter, we will focus on four facets of this liturgical spirit that can help us grow closer to God and deepen our discipleship through our service on the liturgy committee.

---

7. SC, 28.
8. SC, 29.
9. SC, 29

A spirit of collaboration is at the heart of the ministry of the liturgy committee.

God's Work and Our Work

The word *liturgy* comes from a Greek word, *leitourgia*, which means "public work" or "work of the people." And the liturgy *is* work! It is not a passive activity; rather, it calls on us to participate with heart, mind, and voice. It demands preparation, both spiritual and practical. It calls on us to use our minds, to learn and study and plan. It draws on our gifts: gifts of voice and music, of speaking, writing, and hospitality. All of this is important work. But it is not the most important work that happens during the liturgy. At the beginning of *Sacrosanctum concilium*, the Second Vatican Council explains the purpose of the liturgy by quoting an ancient prayer that is still part of the missal today:

> For the liturgy, "making the work of our redemption a present actuality," most of all in the divine sacrifice of the eucharist is the outstanding means whereby the faithful may express their lives and manifest to others the mystery of Christ and the real nature of the true Church.[10]

"The work of our redemption": this is not *our* work but God's saving work in Christ, and it happens in our midst in the celebration of the Mass. Christ is present, and he is anything but passive! In the liturgy, Christ is truly at work. It is Christ who baptizes, Christ who speaks his saving Word, Christ who feeds us with his Body and Blood.

Work of the people, work of redemption: there is no contradiction here. The liturgy is both. The liturgy is, in fact, a collaboration. God invites us to

---

10. SC, 1, quoting the prayer over the gifts from the Evening Mass of the Lord's Supper on Holy Thursday and the Second Sunday in Ordinary Time.

meet him halfway, to do our part in his saving work on our behalf. God does not wait until we have been perfected to invite us into this holy endeavor. God invites us now, with all our limitations, with all our imperfections, with all that we have yet to learn.

The spirit of the liturgy is, therefore, a spirit of collaboration—and that has something to say to liturgy committees since collaboration is at the heart of this ministry. When we are part of a group project and everyone agrees, we might tend to think that we must be doing something right. But, in a sense, true collaboration only begins when we face challenges. And challenges will come. Serving on the liturgy committee is no ivory tower. We seldom—if ever!—sit around the table like rows of angels in an old painting, each playing our instrument in perfect harmony. The liturgy committee is a crash course in learning how to disagree respectfully, how to respond when reality does not live up to our expectations, how to be patient when the "same old same old" is seen as good enough, how to let go and how to hang on. We need to recognize these challenging moments for what they are: opportunities to learn the holy art of collaboration. If we do not achieve perfect unanimity, we have not failed. Failure comes when we judge or reject others who may not see eye to eye with us. Failure comes when we get our way by silencing others. Failure comes when we allow ourselves to be silenced because of intimidation or expediency.

The First Letter of St. Paul to the Corinthians is good reading for any group that finds collaboration challenging. Here was a community of fervent Christian believers who could not agree on anything —not even on how to celebrate the Eucharist. St. Paul offers them much wise counsel, including these surprising words:

> Pray, then, come and join this choir, every one of you; let there be a holy symphony of minds in concert; take the tone all together from God, and sing aloud to the Father with one voice through Jesus Christ, so that he may hear you and know by your good works that you are indeed members of his Son's Body.
>
> —St. Ignatius of Antioch

> I hear that when you meet as a church there are divisions among you, and to a degree I believe it; there have to be factions among you in order that (also) those who are approved among you may become known.[11]

To say that "there have to be factions"[12] is not to say that each person is entitled to their opinion, or that every viewpoint is equally right. Far from it! St. Paul is pointing out that disagreements serve a vital function in a Christian community. Disagreements lead to discussion and debate, and these can lead us to clarity of purpose. It is in these disagreeable moments that we learn to collaborate.

---

11. 1 Corinthians 11:18–19.
12. 1 Corinthians 11:18.

Questions for Discussion and Reflection

1. Collaboration is a key part of service on a liturgy committee. Think about a rewarding experience of collaboration you have had, whether at work, school, or in another parish ministry. What made it rewarding?

2. How might what you experienced there shape your contribution to the Liturgy Committee in your parish?

The Holiness of Time

The Catholic liturgy unfolds in time. Easter is the high point of the year, the day of days around which the whole year revolves. In the cycle of seasons, "the church unfolds the whole mystery of Christ," and thus "opens to the faithful the riches of the Lord's powers and merits, so that these are in some way made present in every age in order that the faithful may lay hold on them and be filled with saving grace."[13] Through the rhythm of times and seasons, the whole mystery of Christ, from his incarnation to his resurrection to his second coming, is proclaimed and even made present among us.

That same pattern is echoed every week: Sunday is our weekly Easter, a day set apart to celebrate the resurrection of Christ. And each day of the week is marked with prayer, not only by the celebration of daily Mass but by the Liturgy of the Hours, the prayer of the Church, which (as its name implies) offers every part of the day to God.

Through the liturgy, the passing of time is made holy. And through the liturgy, time is also put in its proper perspective because we know that "with the Lord one day is like a thousand years and a thousand years like one day."[14] Whenever we celebrate the Mass, we step into a different way of measuring time because the liturgy, while it unfolds in the present, unites us with eternity. "Grant that, with you as our ruler and guide, / we may use the good things that pass / in such a way as to hold fast even now / to those that ever endure" we pray in the collect for the Seventeenth Sunday in Ordinary Time. Although we live among passing things, through our worship, we are already grasping those realities that last forever. In the liturgy, earth meets heaven and time touches eternity: our prayer is joined to the prayers of those who already look at the face of God. This is the spirit of the liturgy: *time is holy.*

The liturgy committee spends a lot of time reflecting on time. That sounds like an odd thing to say, but it is true: our meetings are spent planning the unfolding of the parish's liturgical life in time! From Advent and Christmas to Lent, Easter, and the long stretches of Ordinary Time, we work to let the distinct character of each season shine through in the way the liturgy is

---

13. SC, 102.
14. 2 Peter 3:8.

celebrated. And within the liturgy itself, we seek to make every moment count through the music we sing, the readings we hear, and the silence we keep. Given this emphasis on time in our ministry, our spirituality should also be infused with an awareness of time. What would that look like?

We can find some answers in *Dies Domini*, an apostolic letter that was issued in 1998. In this wonderful letter, Pope St. John Paul II reflects on the challenges to keeping Sunday holy in our modern lives. More and more people are required to work on Sundays, and working from home blurs the boundaries between time on and time off. And the weekend—a relatively recent concept!—alters, without really slowing down, the rhythm of life. All these realities can make Mass on Sunday more challenging for people, including ourselves.

But participation in Sunday Mass is more than Church law; it is a gift. When we set aside time for God in this way, we recognize that Christ is indeed the Lord of time and of history. And, as the pope observes, Sunday is not just the Lord's Day. Sunday is also *our* day. He calls it *Dies ecclesiae*, Day of the Church, a day to receive the Body of Christ in the Eucharist, and to recognize ourselves and others as the Body of Christ, active and living in the world. And the Day of the Church is also *Dies hominis*, the Day of humanity. Our rest from work is not just for our personal benefit. Through this rest, we can reflect on the meaning and importance of work, and grow in solidarity with those who have no work and with those whose work is burdensome. Sunday is thus both a day of rest and an invitation to justice. Taking a step out of our daily pattern by keeping Sunday holy gives us time and space to *see* the struggles and cares of the world. "In Christianity," Pope St. John Paul II has written, "time has a fundamental importance. . . . In Jesus Christ, the Word made flesh, time becomes a dimension of God, who is himself eternal."[15]

> O humdrum days . . . I look upon you with a solemn and festive eye. How great and solemn is the time that gives us the chance to gather merits for eternal heaven! I understand how the saints made use of it.
>
> —St. Faustina Kowalska

Time is a dimension of God! As members of the liturgy committee, we should pay special attention to how we spend our time, especially how we spend our Sundays. Is Sunday truly a day of rest, a day of the Lord, a day of the Church, and a day of humanity for us? Or does Sunday become just another a busy day, a lopsided day, with competing priorities? Achieving that balance is no easy task, but it is an important one. Indeed, as liturgy committee members, our primary task is to help the parish keep Sunday—and how can we do that unless we have discovered the mystery of Sunday for ourselves?

---

15. *Dies Domini*, 74.

Questions for Discussion and Reflection

1. How do you spend your time?

2. Do you feel you have a good balance in your life between parish, work, and family?

3. What does Sunday look like in your life?

Imbued with the Spirit of the Liturgy
Looking Inward

Whenever we turn on the TV, flip through the pages of a magazine, or open a social media app, we are likely to be are inundated with words and images that seem chaotic, even random; however, those words and images present a fairly consistent view of our place in the world. They insist that we are here to live pleasant lives in beautiful, pain-free bodies for as long as we possibly can, all through consumption of the right products. This stream of advertising con-stantly challenges us to examine our possessions and ourselves, but this self-examination stays very much on the surface.

The liturgy reminds us that Christ became human, and in so doing, opened the way for us to share in the divine nature.

The worldview in which the liturgy immerses us is totally different. At the beginning of Mass we acknowledge our sinfulness in the penitential act, and then immediately sing God's praises in the Gloria. It is a pattern that is repeated again and again during the Mass—think of the Communion Rite, for example, in which we pray "Lord, I am not worthy" and then process forward to receive Communion. The liturgy reminds us who we are, and who God is.

Of course, that is not the whole story. We are sinners, yes, but through Christ, we have become much more than that. As we pray in one of the prefaces of Christmas Time, "when our frailty is assumed by your Word / not only does human mortality receive unending honor / but by this wondrous union we, too, are made eternal."[16] The liturgy reminds us that Christ became human, and in so doing, opened the way for us to share in the divine nature.

We are dust, but we are also eternal. This is our Christian worldview in a nutshell. If we recall the first chapter of the Book of Genesis, we read that

---

16. Preface III of the Nativity of the Lord.

human beings were created in the divine image. In the second chapter of Genesis, we learn that they were taken from the dust. And by the third chapter, their short stay in Eden is over! There is a sense of whiplash in this, and yet it rings true. Dignity and dust, sacredness and sin are all realities of the human condition, and very often are at work in us at the same moment.

These dual realities of the human condition are constantly at work in the liturgy as well. In the words of the Exsultet, the Easter Proclamation, "O truly necessary sin of Adam, / destroyed completely by the Death of Christ! / O happy fault / that earned so great, so glorious a Redeemer!" The sin of Adam and Eve was "necessary" because it became the means by which God's surpassing mercy in Christ was poured out upon the world. Through the "amazing mystery" of Christ's redeeming death and resurrection, our fallen nature is not simply repaired but restored "to yet greater dignity than at its beginnings."[17] St. Paul said it this way: "where sin increased, grace overflowed all the more."[18]

The liturgy presents a Christian vision of the place of human beings in the universe.

The liturgy reveals Christ to us; it also reveals *us* to us. The liturgy presents a Christian vision of the place of human beings in the universe. We are simultaneously less important and more important than we think we are! The purpose of liturgy is not to make us feel good about ourselves; rather, the liturgy gives us a glimpse of the real nature of things. The liturgy both reassures and challenges us. The spirit of the liturgy is, therefore, a spirit of honest self-knowledge.

As members of the liturgy committee, called to be imbued with the spirit of the liturgy, we need to heed the liturgy's reminder to know who we are, our strengths as well as our weaknesses. This self-awareness will make us more effective members of the committee. It can also open our eyes to the giftedness of others and help us make room for new voices and new ideas when we get too comfortable with the old ones. It can help us acknowledge honestly when we fail in charity toward each other and move on with our bonds restored and strengthened. Knowledge of our own limitations should give us compassion for the limitations of others; and remembering how precious we are in God's sight should give us the courage to share our gifts and contribute actively to the ministry to which we have been called.

---

17. Collect for Thursday of the Fourth Week of Easter.
18. Romans 5:20.

Looking Outward

The church building is a place set apart for worship, and when we celebrate the liturgy, we enter a time set apart. But even as we consecrate spaces and times for worship, the liturgy never turns its back on the world. Our parish churches stand not in a wilderness but in the midst of a specific community: among the homes and workplaces of ordinary people, some Catholic, some not, carrying on the ordinary business of their lives. And when we come to the liturgy, we do not leave our own sorrows and struggles at the door. We could not do that even if we tried! And that is not what the liturgy asks of us, for whenever we truly encounter Christ, everything in us comes to the surface. Think of Jesus' conversation with the Samaritan woman at the well. She thinks they are talking about whether the right place to worship is in Jerusalem or elsewhere, but soon they are discussing her relationship with God, and everything she has done (including her five husbands!) comes into their dialogue. The same should happen when we come to Mass. We are not entering a hermetically sealed room, leaving everything we brought with us at the door. We are simply talking with Jesus in the midst of our busy, joyful, stressful, messy, disappointing, hopeful lives, bringing with us all that we are, and the world of which we are a part.

We call the liturgy "source" and "summit."[19] It is the "source" because it is from the celebration of the liturgy, particularly the Eucharist, that the Church draws the grace to carry on the mission of Christ. The liturgy is also the "summit toward which the activity of the Church is directed,"[20] since all that we do is ultimately oriented towards gathering the whole world around one table to share in the feast of faith. The liturgy is dynamic. We are gathered together as a community, we are nourished with God's Word and fed with the Body and Blood of Christ, and then we are sent forth again. Through our participation, through our reception of word and sacrament, we are to be transformed. If we listen carefully to the prayer after Communion at Mass, we will hear, week after week, a prayer for our own transformation and a renewal of our commitment to live differently because of what we have received:

> Govern by your Spirit, we pray, O Lord,
> those you feed with the Body and Blood of your Son,
> that, professing you not just in word or in speech,
> but also in works and in truth,
> we may merit to enter the Kingdom of Heaven.[21]

Although the Eucharist is a foretaste of heaven, it is no rubber stamp on a passport. When we receive the Eucharist, we commit ourselves to *living* Christ,

---

19. SC, 10; LG, 11.
20. SC, 10.
21. Prayer after Communion, Ninth Sunday in Ordinary Time.

not just talking about him. The Eucharist binds us to work for unity in the Church,[22] to "pass from former ways to newness of life,"[23] to be conformed to Christ's image,[24] "to serve you in our neighbor,"[25] to let the Eucharist, "not our own desires," prevail in our lives.[26] Our participation in the Eucharist fills us with heavenly grace and then sends us forth to share that grace here and now, to glorify the Lord by the way we live our lives.

The liturgy committee is a big part of making liturgy happen in the parish. We prepare carefully by bringing all our intelligence and creativity to bear upon helping the parish celebrate the liturgy fully, consciously, and actively. We envision a community united in song, fervent in prayer, listening

> **The glory of God is a living person; and the life of the person consists in beholding God.**
>
> —St. Irenaeus

and responding and understanding what they are doing. Our task is to imagine the liturgy coming to life in our parish as never before. But of course, liturgy really *happens* when it comes to life not inside but outside of the walls of the church. Full, conscious, and active participation is not something we can measure in decibels! True participation happens when we integrate the liturgy into our daily lives—when we bring the realities of our world with us when we pray, and when, in turn, we take the reality of the Eucharist, Christ's living presence among us, into the world we live in through our actions of love and solidarity.

The spirit of the liturgy is thus not separation from the world, but engagement with and transformation of the world, starting with ourselves. This is what it means to say that "the Eucharist commits us to the poor."[27] The liturgy opens our eyes to who we are. It should also open our eyes to the needs around us; otherwise, we will find ourselves caught up in contradiction. As St. John Chrysostom said long ago:

> You dishonor this table when you do not judge worthy of sharing your food someone judged worthy to take part in this meal. . . . God freed you from all your sins and invited you here, but you have not become more merciful.[28]

The liturgy is, in short, anything but private. As Pope Benedict XVI has written:

> Union with Christ is also union with all those to whom he gives himself. I cannot possess Christ just for myself; I can belong to him only in union

---

22. See collect, Eleventh Sunday in Ordinary Time.
23. Prayer after Communion, Sixteenth Sunday in Ordinary Time.
24. See Prayer after Communion, Twentieth Sunday in Ordinary Time.
25. Prayer after Communion, Twenty-Second Sunday in Ordinary Time.
26. Prayer after Communion, Twenty-Fourth Sunday in Ordinary Time.
27. CCC, 1397.
28. Quoted in CCC, 1397.

with all those who have become, or who will become, his own. Communion draws me out of myself towards him, and thus also towards unity with all Christians.[29]

To be united with Christ in the Eucharist is to be united with all those whom Christ loves. And that means, in a special way, those who are poor, afflicted, or in any kind of need. The liturgy calls us to share with those who lack the basic necessities of life and to be in solidarity with those deprived of peace and justice. As members of the liturgy committee, we have a double responsibility: to live the spirit of the liturgy in our own lives and to help the parish celebrate the liturgy in such a way that others can do the same.

Questions for Discussion and Reflection

1. The liturgy invites us to look at ourselves through God's eyes, to know what it means to be human. What do you see as your weaknesses and strengths?

2. How might knowing your weaknesses and strengths help you to serve more effectively on the liturgy committee?

3. The liturgy invites us to look outward. Is church an escape for me?

4. Am I comfortable with the liturgy's call to transformation, both for myself and for the world we live in?

5. Am I ready to step outside the doors of the parish and work for the building up of the kingdom of God?

---

29. *Deus caritas est*, 14.

Chapter Five

Frequently Asked Questions

1. What is the proper way to refer to the name of the committee? Liturgy, worship, committee, commission, or board?

In some parishes this organization might be called a *liturgy commission*, or *worship committee* or *commission* or even *board*. Although these words have similarities, there are some differences worth noting. The *Merriam-Webster's Collegiate Dictionary* defines *committee* as "a body of persons delegated to consider, investigate, take action on, or report on some matter."[1] *Commission* is defined as "a group of persons directed to perform some duty"[2] (such as the Vatican Commission for COVID-19[3]). That same resource defines a *board* as "a group of persons having managerial, supervisory, investigatory, or advisory powers" such as "board of directors."[4] Looking at those three words, *committee* and *commission* most closely speaks of the group representing the various liturgical ministries acting as an advisory or decision-making body for all. *Commission* tends to be a more formal designation; so for the purposes of this work, *committee* is used throughout.

The liturgy committee acts as an advisory board to the parish.

The word *worship* is defined as "to honor or reverence as a divine being or supernatural power."[5] *Liturgy*, in its broadest sense, means "the work of the people" or "the official public worship of the Church." A strict definition of *liturgy* implies that the work of the committee is focused on the official rites and rituals of the Church. This would not include public devotions such as the Stations of the Cross or additional prayer services. Certainly, the work of the committee is broader and concerns the entire prayer life of the parish. There really is no error in being called a liturgy committee or a worship committee—it's more of an issue of semantics and precise terminology. Because it is more common for Catholic parishes to refer to this committee as a *liturgy commitee*, this term has been used throughout this book. In the end, how you are identified may depend on

---

1. *Merriam-Webster's Collegiate Dictionary*, 11th ed. (2006), s.v. "committee," 1a.
2. *Merriam-Webster's Collegiate Dictionary*, 11th ed. (2006), s.v. "commission," 1.4a.
3. See this page to reference the work of this commission: https://www.vaticannews.va/en/vatican
-city/news/2020-07/vatican-commission-covid-19-more-money-healthcare-less-weapons.html.
4. *Merriam-Webster's Collegiate Dictionary*, 11th ed. (2006), s.v. "board," 1.3e1.
5. *Merriam-Webster's Collegiate Dictionary*, 11th ed. (2006), s.v. "worship," 2.1.

your diocese and the terminology they use, not to mention that which has been customary in your parish community.

2. In what other ways should members of the liturgy committee be involved in the parish? Should all of them be liturgical ministers? Or just actively participating in the pews?

In general, liturgy committees tend to include chairpersons from the various liturgical ministries: the readers, extraordinary ministers of holy Communion, hospitality ministers, and so on, along with clergy representation and any salaried liturgical staff. These representatives are already knowledgeable about their area of liturgy and bring that information to the table. When a topic affects their ministry, they can provide input and likewise communicate as necessary with their ministers.

However, not everyone on the committee needs to be a liturgical minister. One or two can be people who represent the assembly, the active participants in the pew. These individuals are not focused on a specific ministerial area. Because they are looking through different lenses, they often bring a fresh perspective to committee's work. They can help gauge how well the assembly will embrace what is up for consideration. They will keep the group grounded and focused on its ultimate goal of providing a good liturgical experience for the people.

3. How do we maintain an open and friendly relationship with the assembly without being perceived as the liturgy police?

An open and friendly relationship with the assembly means creating an atmosphere where people feel genuinely welcomed and where they are encouraged to fully participate as called for in *Sacrosanctum concilium*.[6] In other words, the quality of hospitality must be evident throughout the liturgy. What might that look like?

When there are new Mass parts or a new Communion song, do you just hope and pray that the assembly will catch on? Hopefully not. Take a few minutes before Mass begins, over the period of several weeks, to introduce the assembly to the new Mass parts. As you rehearse each week, affirm how well they are doing.

Perhaps you need to change the route for your Communion procession. You will want to make sure you give the people advance notice—one or two weeks. You may even want to model the change to avoid unnecessary distractions during the Communion Rite. These are small but significant efforts. They say to people that you want them to have a good experience of prayer, one in which they can easily participate. Even the placement of seasonal environment can welcome participation. Are we only placing flowers and hangings in the

---

6. See SC, 14–20.

sanctuary where the ordained sit? Can some of these symbols find a home in the assembly's space to show the importance of their role.

As a liturgy committee, strive to love the assembly as you love yourselves. Strive to treat them with the dignity and respect each person deserves. This means preparing the assembly through catechesis, giving advance notice when necessary, and offering appreciation for their role. Theirs is the most important liturgical ministry, as they become bread for the those who hunger, pour out their lives in sacrifice, and bring the Good News to home, workplace, and beyond.

4. How do we implement best practice changes in a respectful way?

Even when change is inevitable, most people may have a strong desire to keep things the same. When this is the case regarding a parish custom that is not in tune with good liturgy, change can be even more difficult. Many view the Church as a constant in their life. *If we start changing the way we pray, what's left?* they may think. While keeping this in mind, the liturgy committee still has a responsibility to carry out liturgical directives found in the liturgical documents or directed by the Holy See, the United States bishops, or the diocese.

To navigate such clashes with grace, consider the following. Do not hurry the process. Take the time to understand the attachment to the custom. Listen to all sides for what is important. For example, if this is a ritual that is not appropriate for the Sunday liturgy, can it be effectively incorporated into a prayer service instead? If it is something that obscures the altar and distracts from prayer (such as a crèche in front of the altar), can we together find a suitable place for this beloved sign?

In these discussions, make certain that everyone's opinion and point of view is heard and recorded without passing judgment. Then sit back and look for common ground that might point toward a solution. Welcome divergent opinions as they often stimulate creative options that otherwise might not have been explored. Continue to dialogue, revisit the decision, and review how well the change is being accepted.

5. Our pastor ignores our work. What should we do?

This is an important question that needs to be resolved through ongoing dialogue. On the one hand, whoever is directing liturgy in the parish needs to have an open and honest discussion with the pastor regarding his expectations for the group. What does he want from the group, and what are the parameters? On the other hand, if there is something the committee wants to do that is legitimate, ask him to at least hear you out. It is hoped that such discussions will get you to a point where the pastor begins to value the group's contribution to parish life and that the liturgy committee will feel appreciated.

Keep communication open and show charity to others.

You may have to lower your expectations for a time. Be sure to clarify what he is willing to have you do. Do those tasks and do them well. As the pastor sees what the group is able to accomplish, he is more likely to broaden the scope of your work.

Are you a decision-making body or an advisory group? That question needs clarification as well. When an issue comes up for discussion, it is helpful for the pastor to identify the role of the group. Right from the beginning, the group needs to know whether they are making a recommendation or they are actually making a final decision.

Keep communication open, otherwise you will be setting yourself up for frustration. When it comes to group work, no one wants to waste time; everyone wants to be appreciated for their contribution. But when there is lack of clarity, group members become discouraged, and the group will most likely disband or gradually fall apart.

6. How do we handle complaints or requests from the assembly (or even from another committee member)?

Complaints and disapproval of the committee's work can be hard to take, especially when what is being criticized falls within the boundaries of good liturgical practice. It can be tempting to respond immediately by explaining why we do this or that, and by attempting to defend the decision. Instead, take a deep breath and listen. Most of the time, people just want to know that someone actually heard them without brushing them off. As you listen, try to hear what might be behind the critique. An empathic response might be in order. For example, the person might be complaining that there is little organ music and too much contemporary music. You might respond, "It sounds like you're really missing your old community where you heard the organ every Sunday."

You can commiserate about how difficult changes can be. And while this may not solve everything, it will go a long way to fostering understanding.

If the complaint is legitimate, you might invite the person to share his or her observations during one of your monthly meetings. This is not a "solve the problem" session, but a time to listen. If you find that you are getting a number of complaints on the same issue, from the assembly or even from a committee member, it could mean that more formation and further study of the liturgical documents are needed to properly respond to the situation and implement a good change.

Remember to thank people who complain for coming forward and trusting you to hear them. Let them know that such discussions are opportunities for you to learn as well. It may not seem like it, but those who complain love their communities as much as you do—a foundation on which to build.

7. How does the committee handle a new pastor when the vision or personal spirituality of the pastor is quite different from the vision of the parish?

Move slowly and thoughtfully when there is new leadership in the parish. Resolve to exercise Christian hospitality, the hallmark of every disciple of Jesus. Welcome the new pastor as you would welcome Christ and as you would like to be welcomed. Begin with a nonthreatening event like a casual dinner in someone's home. Get to know him and let him become acquainted with all of you. Do all this before you start discussing any liturgical practices.

Next, share what you have accomplished during the past year by providing him with minutes from the last months. Share your parish's vision for liturgy. Ask him about his former parish and how they worshipped. What are his observations of the way your community prays? As you listen, look for signs of common ground. Where can you begin to work together?

Collaborative ministry is all about relationship building, and relationships take time to develop. It takes time for people to trust one another. So determine which issues are most important. Where will you need to exercise patience and temporarily put aside parts of the vision? There will be those areas where you will have to agree to disagree and leave it at that. And there will be goals you will not be able to achieve. No one said this would always be easy!

A change in leadership is a challenge for everyone: the parish as a whole, the liturgy committee, and the new pastor. Try to keep an open mind. And who knows? You may end up "entertaining angels."[7]

---

7. Hebrews 13:2.

8. What is the best way to solicit the assembly's opinion on the liturgy?

A survey is a valuable tool to gather information from a large number of people. Once survey findings are collated, they can assist a liturgy committee in making informed decisions. However, before you consider any kind of a survey, be clear on your objective. What do you really want to know, and how will you use what you have learned? As you design your survey, be certain to phrase your questions so they do not lead to preconceived conclusions.

If you are looking for a broad base of opinions, you will probably want the survey to go to all registered parishioners. How will you accomplish that? Email and such services as Survey Monkey are viable options, though not everyone uses email. Will you put the survey in the bulletin or have it available in your gathering area or the parish office?

When creating a survey, less is more. Most people shy away from anything beyond one page. Ask clear questions where they can share their opinions on a scale of 1 to 5 (strongly disagree to strongly agree). Then allow space for those being surveyed to write in comments and for the option to share name and contact information.

Beyond a parish survey, and depending on your objective, you might conduct focus groups. Bring lectors and readers together one night, ministers of hospitality on another, and so on. These small group discussions can be very productive when people are energized by each other's input. One verbalized idea can spark another. The success of a focus group will depend on a good facilitator and someone who can accurately record everyone's contributions.

9. How does the committee make decisions? How can the tone of discussions be kept comfortable? How can we build trust and relationships on the committee?

Ideally, decisions are best made by consensus: every single person arrives at agreements and solutions that everyone can live with, although everyone might not agree with every part of the decision. Unlike a simple vote, reaching consensus takes more work and more time as you listen to one another and carefully weigh what is best for your congregation. But it is time well spent. Thoughtful discussions tend to bear good fruit. Voting, on the other hand, can be divisive, especially if there are some noticeable divisions in the group.

Consensus works best when those involved feel comfortable expressing their viewpoint. So before making major decisions, the one who is in charge should set the tone by making two important reminders: (1) restate clearly the issue that is being decided, and (2) remind them that "who says what" should stay within the group. Next, all should be able to disagree without being disagreeable. If someone's idea is criticized too sharply, it is unlikely that others will be comfortable sharing. Communication may actually shut down. Trust grows when it is watered with kindness and a heart that listens. Charity and love must prevail throughout the process.

Additionally, if you are working on a goal where the pastor will ultimately make the decision, everyone should know that up front. Are you actually making the decision, or are you acting as an advisory body?

It is worth noting that a liturgy committee does not need to make every liturgical decision. The principle of subsidiarity should hold sway: to make decisions at the lowest possible level. Thus, some tasks can be delegated to another more appropriate group. Liturgy committees do not have to select every type of flower for the Easter season. Nor do they need to decide when lectors and readers will be trained. Leave that to those with leadership positions.

10. How does the committee become informed about the diocesan worship office's policies and cultivate a relationship?

Besides preparing diocesan liturgies, diocesan offices exist to assist parishes in their ongoing responsibility of providing good liturgy. Therefore, they offer some or all of the following services: ministerial workshops, certification programs in liturgy, parish Mass evaluations, consultations tailored to the needs of the committee, and even lending libraries (of books and DVDs). They answer questions and provide reassurance. Clearly, you want to keep informed about their offerings and cultivate a good relationship.

Your awareness of the diocesan worship office's services often depends on the lines of communication within your parish. Correspondence with diocesan offices often ends up on the pastor's desk, where it may not always get his immediate attention. Offices of worship will also communicate with part- or full-time liturgical staff. These staff members should be passing on pertinent information to the liturgy committee when they meet.

But what if you are a volunteer liturgy coordinator? Pick up the phone or send an email, introduce yourself, and get on their mailing list. If possible, invite the director of the diocesan office or someone from the diocesan liturgy board to one of your meetings. That person will probably enjoy being in a parish atmosphere to meet with the people who do this important work week after week. At the same time, your group will be enhanced by their presence and knowledge.

11. How might we recruit members from the different cultures of the parish?

Begin by looking to those who are seen as leaders within the different cultural groups. You may be able to observe them at your Sunday liturgies or social gatherings. Then find out whether anyone on your liturgy committee has a relationship with people of other cultures.

Next, be clear on why you want to recruit them. What is it you hope to achieve by their involvement? The hope is that you believe their presence will enrich your group, which will then spill over into the parish itself. We are both a diverse nation and a diverse Church. As James Joyce wrote about the Catholic Church: "Here comes everybody." That diversity needs to be reflected in our ministries and in our leadership roles.

At one of your meetings, look at the minister rosters, and brainstorm about who might be a good fit, keeping the diversity of your committee particularly in mind. If, for example, you have a large Filipino community, but there aren't Filipinos on your committee, invite a representative to serve so that you can ensure that their voice is heard. That person, too, can help you recruit more Filipinos for ministry in the parish.

If the candidate is reluctant to serve on the committee, invite them to a meeting to come see what you do. They may have no idea what you are about and may need some introduction to what a liturgy board is all about. Above all, let them know all are welcome!

The liturgy committee should be aware of the parish's cultural celebrations. Shown here is Simbang Gabi.

12. How can the committee learn parish customs?

Liturgy committees need to be educated not only about liturgy, but also about the legitimate parish customs that have shaped the community over the years. If some current members are also longtime parishioners, anecdotes have probably been shared already. But what if no longtime parishioners are part of your group?

Invite longtime parishioners to attend a liturgy committee meeting to share stories of the parish's liturgical customs. Some may even have pictures to share with the group. Besides information, there can be other positive outcomes of such a meeting. Usually, people love to be asked to share their stories. In some cases, these longtimers are from the elderly population in the parish. They might not be able to remain active in ministry, but they still have much to share. Imagine how they will feel when their wisdom and recollections are valued by the group, plus the liturgy committee grows in knowledge of the community they are called to serve. Everyone wins!

Consider as well that some of these longtimers might have conditions that prevent them from getting to a meeting. After identifying the ones you want to hear from, assign committee members to interview different individuals.

Reports could be done in one meeting or shared one at a time over a period of several months.

Producing a video of the interview would add an interesting dimension to the presentation. If so, such videos could be played on a monitor in your narthex or community room. Besides your group, the praying community would have an opportunity to hear from these wisdom figures.

13. What is the ordo, and how do I use it?

Usually the sacristan or the presider will set up the books and pull out the proper vestments. However, in case you need to help the sacristan or take over in his or her absence, it is good to be familiar with the ordo and how it is used.

The *ordo* (Latin for "order") is a liturgical almanac, published annually. You will need to use the ordo that is specific to your diocese or religious community. The ordo includes an entry for every day of the liturgical year, and includes all the information you need to prepare for the Mass. It tells you the liturgical color of the day, it explains where to find the readings and the presidential prayers, and it includes notes about the Liturgy of the Hours. It also includes a variety of options—optional memorials of the saints, for example, as well as special observances like the World Day of Prayer for the Sick. Some ordos include other useful information, like the pope's prayer intentions for each month, and the local necrology—that is, the list of names of deceased clergy. The shorthand the ordo uses can take some getting used to, but once you get the hang of it you will find it an invaluable resource for preparing for the liturgy.

14. How do I use *The Roman Missal*?

Sometimes before Mass you might be asked to put the ribbons of *The Roman Missal* in the right pages. Your local ordo will point you in the right direction. Let's take a couple of examples.

It's the Second Sunday of Advent. Use one ribbon to mark the "proper" prayers—that is, the prayers unique to this day in the liturgical calendar. You will find them at the beginning of *The Roman Missal*, in the Proper of Time. Use another ribbon to mark the preface. You'll find the prefaces in the center of *The Roman Missal* within the Order of Mass. There are two Advent prefaces. Notice that the second is used only from December 17 to 24. That means you'll want to mark preface I of Advent for today.

What else should be marked in *The Roman Missal*? It depends on local custom and the needs of the priest. It may be that another ribbon could be used to mark the penitential act for the day, either the Confiteor, or perhaps one of the sets of invocations found in appendix VI. Some priests like to have the prayers for the preparation of the altar marked as well. You'll find those at the center of *The Roman Missal*, just after the creed. (A helpful hint: fold the ribbons you are not using and tuck them out of sight, leaving visible only the ribbons that will be used during the current Mass. This will help prevent unnecessary flipping of pages.)

It's June 5, the memorial of St. Boniface. You find his prayers in Proper of Saints for June 5. But you notice right away that only one prayer, the collect, is provided. So after you mark that page, you'll want to mark the rest of the prayers in one of the commons. A note suggests using either "For One Martyr," from the Common of Martyrs, or "For Missionaries," from the Common of Pastors, because St. Boniface was a missionary who carried the Gospel to the people of Germany. You might mark both of them, and let the priest decide which set he prefers.

Having marked the prayers, you next need to mark the preface. Again, there are two options—you can mark one of the two prefaces of holy martyrs or the Preface of Holy Pastors.

It's the Third Sunday of Lent, and the first scrutiny of the elect is being celebrated. There are two options for the prayers. You can mark the prayers for the Third Sunday of Lent in the Proper of Time, or you can mark the prayers for the scrutinies in the section Ritual Masses. Either set of prayers may be used when a scrutiny is celebrated. Ask the priest which he prefers.

If the scrutiny of the elect is being celebrated in your parish, that means that the readings for year A are being used as well. So you will want to mark the proper preface for the Third Sunday of Lent, which is only used when the Gospel of the Woman of Samaria is read. Notice that this preface is found in the Proper of Time along with the other prayers for the Third Sunday of Lent. In years B or C, when no scrutiny is celebrated, one of the general Lenten prefaces should be used. These are found in the Order of Mass.

15. How do I use the Sunday and weekday lectionaries?

You might need to mark the pages in the various lectionaries for the reader and the presider. To mark the readings for a Sunday Mass, you need to know whether you are in year A, year B, or year C. Here is a quick guide to the lectionary for the next few years. Notice that the lectionary year begins with the First Sunday of Advent, which usually falls in late November or very early December, and ends with the Solemnity of Our Lord Jesus Christ, King of the Universe, in late November of the following year.

	Sunday	Weekday
Advent 2020–Christ the King 2021	Year B	I
Advent 2021–Christ the King 2022	Year C	II
Advent 2022–Christ the King 2023	Year A	I

Once you know which year of the lectionary you are in, it is easy to mark the Sunday lectionary. You'll notice that every Sunday is assigned a distinctive number. This is very helpful as these numbers are unique to each set of readings. If the local ordo tells you that the Sunday readings for today can be found at #60B, you'll find only one set of readings with that number no matter how many volumes of the lectionary you thumb through—#60B refers to the readings for the Seventh Sunday of Easter in year B.

After marking the Sunday lectionary for the readers, you'll want to mark the *Book of the Gospels* for the deacon or priest. The number you used to find the readings in the Sunday lectionary will help you find the appropriate Gospel as well.

It is helpful to place the lectionary in a consistent place in the sacristy where the readers can review it before Mass. They will have prepared for their reading at home, but it is always good for them to see the words on the actual page they will be reading from. After the readers have had a chance to look at the lectionary, the book can be placed at the ambo. The *Book of the Gospels* should similarly be placed where the priest or deacon can review the reading before Mass.

The weekday readings are on a two-year cycle—year I and year II. As a general rule, the readings for year I are read in odd calendar years, and year II in even calendar years. Keep in mind, though, that the liturgical year begins with Advent, so you will move into year I at the end of an even year, like 2022, and then back into year II toward the end of 2023.

During Advent, Christmas Time, Lent, and Easter Time, the weekday readings are the same in both year I and year II. During Ordinary Time, the Gospel is the same but the first reading and the responsorial psalm are different. Note also that the lectionary numbers don't always help you here. If you go to #379, you will find the readings and psalms for both year I and year II. Double check the ordo to find out whether you want the story of Hagar (year I) from the Book of Genesis or the harsh words of the prophet Amos (year II)! Most lectionaries will provide additional help by indicating year I or year II in the heading before the first reading and responsorial psalm.

Here are some examples to help you navigate through the lectionary.

- It is the Fourth Sunday of Lent in year B. The parish is celebrating the second scrutiny of the elect. When the scrutinies are celebrated, the readings for year A are used, no matter what year it is. That means that instead of marking #32B, you'll mark #31A in the Sunday lectionary. You'll also mark the Gospel of the man born blind in the *Book of the Gospels*, also #31A.

- It is Friday of the Nineteenth Week in Ordinary Time. With the help of your local ordo, you find lectionary #417 quite easily. It is year I, so you mark the reading from Joshua instead of the reading from Ezekiel.

- It is Thanksgiving Day, and the priest has chosen special readings: Isaiah 63:7–9, Psalm 138, Colossians 3:12–17, and Luke 17:11–19. How do you find these readings in the lectionary? You could use the Scripture index at the back of the book, which tells you where each Scripture passage is found in the lectionary. Referring to this index, you find that the reading from Isaiah occurs only once in the lectionary, at #943 in "Masses for Various Needs and Occasions." Turning to #943 in the lectionary, you discover that the priest has chosen all the readings from among the many options given for Masses "In Thanksgiving to God" under "Various Needs and Occasions." From here, it is easy to find and mark the other readings that have been chosen.

16. How can we help members of the assembly to participate better and to recognize that the Sunday Mass is the most important thing they do each week?

Your parish can encourage participation by complimenting parishioners when they do it well. You can also work harder at building the parish community by helping people to become better acquainted. When individual worshippers feel welcomed into the community and comfortable with one another, they relax, sing better, and enjoy their time at the liturgy. They offer more fitting praise to God through their mutual concern for one another.

The parish leadership should also take a hard look at the budget for music. Offering better salaries can attract better musicians. When the music improves, people participate better in offering praise to God.

Musicians will help if they truly practice the music for Mass and come prepared to lead. Good preaching will help people realize the significance of their time together each Sunday. They will grow more aware of their faith and discover ways to put it into practice. Good worship will help Catholics become better Christians all week long, and their practice of the faith will enhance their worship.

17. How can the liturgy committee be attentive to the cultural dynamic in the parish?

God's people come in a wide variety of colors, ethnic backgrounds, and cultures. If your parish has such diversity, it is both a blessing and a challenge. Although you find yourself enriched by the multicultural aspects of your community, you may find it daunting to bring together the expectations of varying groups without avoiding conflicts.

If your parish has a large Filipino community, you may be called upon to host a *Simbang Gabi* Mass during the Advent season. Will that take place during a regular weekend liturgy or on a Sunday afternoon? If it takes place at a regularly scheduled Mass, how will this affect the music and the environment? This is when you may want to invite one or two Filipinos (who are in a leadership position) to sit down with the liturgy committee to hear each other's expectations. Similarly, if your community has a large Hispanic population, the Feast of Our Lady of Guadalupe will need your attention. How and when will it be celebrated?

One parish with numerous cultural traditions can also mean environmental challenges. There's only so much room for so many statues and symbols. Look around your worship area including the narthex or adjacent spaces. Could you create a spot where images are rotated, a place that allows two to three people to pray at one time?

You may also find that a cultural tradition will be completely embraced by the entire community. The Altar of the Dead, a Hispanic tradition, has become in some places a way for people of every persuasion to honor their dead with pictures, notes, candles, and such. Clearly, everyone is a winner in this scenario.

The bottom line: no one group has the right to control the parish liturgy even when they are in the majority. It is our Christian duty to work together to develop strong relationships that respect each other's ethnic backgrounds. Sitting down together, especially over a meal, we can bring fresh understandings. Chances are you will come away surprised at how much common ground you all actually share. The time you spend developing these liturgical relationships will gradually spill over into the entire community.

Resources

Ritual Books

As a member of a liturgy committee, you should know the differences among the various ritual books so that you can learn the Church's vision for the implementation of the rites and reflect upon how they are celebrated in your parish. Listed here are the ritual books of the Church most commonly used in parish settings:

- *Book of Blessings*
- *Book of the Elect*
- *Book of the Gospels*
- *Eucharistic Prayers for Masses with Children*
- *Holy Communion and Worship of the Eucharist Outside Mass*
- *Lectionary for Mass*
- *Lectionary for Mass, Supplement*
- *Lectionary for Masses with Children*
- *Masses of the Blessed Virgin Mary*
- *Rite of Christian Initiation of Adults*
- *Rite of Penance*
- *Order of Baptism of Children*
- *Order of Celebrating Matrimony*
- *Order of Confirmation*
- *Order of Christian Funerals*
- *Order for the Solemn Exposition of the Most Holy Eucharist*
- *Pastoral Care of the Sick: Rites of Anointing and Viaticum*
- *The Roman Missal*
- *Sunday Celebrations in the Absence of a Priest*

Church Documents

As a member of a liturgy committee, you should become familiar with the major liturgical documents from both the Vatican and the United States Conference of Catholic Bishops. These documents are included in LTP's Liturgy Documents series (there are four volumes in this collection).

Built of Living Stones: Art, Architecture, and Worship: This document from the USCCB is intended primarily as a guide to building or renovating churches, but it is useful for all who are involved in the liturgy or in the maintenance of a church building.

Ceremonial of Bishops: This instructional document details how liturgy is to be celebrated with the bishop, dealing specifically with the celebration of Mass. It is the primary reference for discovering the hows and whys of almost any aspect of Eucharistic liturgy.

Directory on Popular Piety and the Liturgy: Principles and Guidelines: This address from Pope John Paul II provides basic guidance for celebrating the devotional life of the Church in a way that is in harmony with the liturgy.

General Instruction of the Roman Missal: The introductory document, or prae-notanda, of *The Roman Missal* that explains the theological background and gives the directions for celebrating the Mass. It both appears at the beginning of *The Roman Missal* and is published separately.

Sacrosanctum concilium: The first constitution promulgated from the Second Vatican Council, this document forms the basis for our communal worship.

Sing to the Lord: Music in Divine Worship: Issued by the United States Conference of Catholic Bishops, approved in 2007, and updated in 2012, this document deals with music in Catholic worship. It addresses music as an integral part of liturgy, and it includes principles for the selection of appropriate music and specific questions concerning music in the rites of the Church.

Ritual Praenotanda: Every ritual book of the Church includes an introduction that provides important theological foundations and explanations for the ritual, along with norms, rubrics, and other instructions.

Theological and Historical Resources

Driscoll, Jeremy S., OSB. *What Happens at Mass,* revised edition. Chicago: Liturgy Training Publications, 2011.

This intelligent, straightforward guide to the Mass concentrates on the ritual form of the liturgy.

Turner, Paul. *Let Us Pray: A Guide to the Rubrics of Sunday Mass.* Updated to conform to the revised English translation of *The Roman Missal.* Collegeville, MN: Pueblo, 2012.

Collating the principle liturgical documents, this book walks the reader through the Mass from start to finish, showing what rubrics pertain to all the different parts. Both scholarly and pastoral, it is a user-friendly resource for those wondering what the rubrics say—and don't say.

Pastoral Resources

Brommer, Joshua R. *Imbued with the Spirit of the Liturgy: Ten Insights from Vatican II's Constitution on the Sacred Liturgy.* Chicago: Liturgy Training Publications, 2013.

This booklet helps readers recognize the deeper insights behind the changes that infuse the liturgy we celebrate today as called for by the first document of the Second Vatican Council. It is the lens through which all subsequent legislation should be interpreted.

DeGrocco, Joseph. *A Pastoral Commentary on the General Instruction of the Roman Missal.* Chicago: Liturgy Training Publications, 2011.

This is an accessible reference for priests and deacons, as well as all liturgical ministers and liturgy committees. It aims at two main goals: (1) to help Catholics reflect more deeply on the meaning of the Mass and the significance of what we do at Mass, and (2) to aid parishes celebrate the Eucharist in a way that is faithful to the norms of the Church and reflective of the goal of fully conscious and active participation envisioned by Sacrosanctum concilium.

Evans, Bernard. *Glorify the Lord by Your Life: Catholic Social Teaching and the Liturgy.* Chicago: Liturgy Training Publications, 2020.

This resource provides a unique approach for understanding the important connection between the liturgy and the seven primary themes of Catholic social teaching. It will inspire you to deepen your relationship with God and with others, to become more aware of the needs of the world, and to recommit yourself to live as Christ's disciples in the world.

Laughlin, Corinna. *The Liturgy: The Source and Summit of Our Christian Life.* Chicago: Liturgy Training Publications, 2019.

This easy-to-read resource explores what it means to call liturgy "source and summit." It will help the Catholic faithful understand the meaning of the liturgy and its importance to our life of faith, experience Christ's four-fold presence in the various Church rites, come to a deeper relationship with God, and reflect on the transforming power of the liturgy to change the world.

Preparing Parish Worship Series: This series from LTP provides in-depth pastoral commentary about the various rites and rituals of the Church. Written by well-known and respected liturgists, these resources will walk you through the many details of the rites.

Sourcebook for Sundays, Seasons, and Weekdays. Chicago: Liturgy Training Publications, annual.

This trusted annual provides concise and helpful material to inspire and assist those who prepare the Mass for each day of the liturgical year.

Turner, Paul. *At the Supper of the Lamb: A Pastoral and Theological Commentary on the Mass.* Chicago: Liturgy Training Publications, 2011.

This resource will help those who prepare the liturgy understand the parts of the Mass so they may enter them more intentionally and prepare for them. Following the Order of Mass as it appears in the third edition of *The Roman Missal*, this resource is an invitation to worship, a call to new intention, a deeper awareness of the privilege we share to be invited to the supper of the Lamb.

Glossary

The following are more basic, general terms that members of liturgy committees should be familiar with. It will be helpful for members of the committee to have access to *A Glossary of Liturgical Terms*, published by Liturgy Training Publications.

Advent: The liturgical time of joyful preparation and anticipation for Christmas. It is also a time of penance, although this aspect is secondary to the spirit of hope-filled waiting. This time, considered to be the start of a new liturgical year, begins on the fourth Sunday before Christmas.

Alb: A full-length white liturgical robe, from the Latin *albus*, meaning white. The alb is the preferred vestment for all ministers, from server to bishop. It recalls the white garment put on at baptism as a sign of putting on the new life of Christ. Ordained ministers wear a stole and an outer garment over the alb.

Ambo: The place from which all the Scripture readings are proclaimed and the homily may be preached during liturgy; a pulpit or lectern. The ambo is also used for the singing of the Exsultet, for announcing the intentions of the universal prayer, and for the leading of the responsorial psalm. The term is derived from a Greek word for "raised place."

Ambry: A place for the storing of the holy oils (chrism, oil of catechumens, and oil of the sick). In older churches the ambry was a niche in the wall, often with a locking door. In new and renovated churches, the ambry is often located near the baptismal font and constructed so that the vessels containing the holy oils can be seen.

Assembly: The people gathered for divine worship, often called the congregation. Contemporary liturgical theology emphasizes that it is the assembly as a whole that celebrates the liturgy under the leadership of a priest.

Bishops' Committee on Divine Worship (BCDW): The department of the United States Conference of Catholic Bishops that assists the bishops in matters related to the liturgy. It is a standing committee made up of bishops, assisted by a group of consultants who are experts in liturgical theology, with an office (secretariat) that carries out the work of the committee.

Blessing: Any prayer that praises and thanks God. In particular, blessing describes those prayers in which God is praised because of some person or object, and thus the individual or object is seen to have become specially dedicated or sanctified because of the prayer of faith. Many blessing prayers ask God's favor toward a person in time of need or on a special occasion. Liturgical celebrations usually conclude with a blessing pronounced over the assembly.

Book of the Gospels: A ritual book from which the passages from the Gospels prescribed for Masses on Sundays, soleminities, feasts of the Lord and of the saints, and ritual Masses are proclaimed; also called an "evangeliary." It may be carried in the entrance procession and placed on the altar, and then processed to the ambo during the Gospel acclamation. It is presented to deacons at their ordination and held over the heads of bishops at their ordination.

Censer: A vessel in which incense is burned on coals; also called a "thrurible." Originally, thuribles were either open bowls, or braziers, that remained stationary or shovel-like containers with handles. Modern thuribles are usually metal vessels with pierced lids that allow air to keep the coals alight. They are suspended by one or more chains and, in the Roman Rite, held midway along the chains while swung toward the object or person being reverenced. In the Eastern Rites, the censer is usually swung at the full-length of the chains.

Chasuble: The outer vestment of priests and bishops worn while celebrating the Eucharist. It is a large, sleeveless garment with a simple opening for the head worn over the stole and alb. The color of the chasuble matches the liturgical color of the feast or liturgical time.

Christmas Time: The period of the liturgical year beginning with Evening Prayer I of the Nativity of the Lord and ending with Evening Prayer on the Feast of the Baptism of the Lord (which may fall on the Sunday or Monday after Epiphany). This liturgical time commemorates the incarnation, the birth of Christ, and his first manifestations.

Commissioning: A term used for the authorizing and blessing of individuals to function as extraordinary ministers of holy Communion. It may also be used in a general sense for the blessing or authorization of laypersons to function in any liturgical ministry.

Concluding Rite: The last part of the Mass, following the Communion Rite. It consists of brief announcements, a greeting, a blessing, and the dismissal of the assembly. If an additional rite follows the Mass, such as the Final Commendation at a funeral or a procession with the Blessed Sacrament, that rite replaces the Concluding Rites of the Mass. The term can also refer to the closing rites in any liturgy.

Conference of Bishops: An official group of bishops in charge of a particular area or territory.

Confiteor: A common name given to the confession of sinfulness used in one form of the penitential act at Mass. The name is derived from the first word of the Latin version, "Confiteor Deo omnipotenti . . ." ("I confess to almighty God . . .").

Congregation for Divine Worship and the Discipline of the Sacraments: One of the departments of the Roman Curia. It has responsibility for all matters relating to the liturgy and sacraments in the Church, performing duties in the name of the pope and with his authority.

Credence Table: The side table on which the vessels and articles needed for the celebration are placed when not in use, particularly during the celebration of the Eucharist.

Dalmatic: The sleeved outer vestment proper to a deacon, worn over the alb and stole. The color of the dalmatic matches the liturgical color of the feast or liturgical time.

Devotions: "This term is used to describe various external practices (e.g., prayers, hymns, observances attached to particular times or places, insignia, medals, habits or customs). Animated by an attitude of faith, such external practices manifest the particular relationship of the faithful with the Divine Persons, or the Blessed Virgin Mary in her privileges of grace and those of her titles which express them, or with the Saints in their configuration with Christ or in their role in the Church's life."[1]

Easter Time: The period of fifty days from the Easter Vigil until the conclusion of Evening Prayer on Pentecost. This liturgical time is celebrated with great joy and exultation as one great feast day, one great Sunday characterized especially by the singing of Alleluia.

Exsultet: The solemn proclamation of the resurrection of Christ that is sung at the Easter Vigil after the procession with the newly lit paschal candle. Ideally it is sung by a deacon, although it may also be sung by the priest celebrant, or a concelebrating priest, or a lay cantor. The Exsultet derives its name from the first word of the Latin text, "rejoice." The authorship of the Exsultet is unknown, but tradition has attributed this great poem of praise to either Ambrose or Augustine.

Feast: A rank within the category of liturgical days, lower than a solemnity but higher than a memorial. Feasts usually do not include Evening Prayer I, but usually do have a complete proper set of texts for the Mass along with readings.

Incense: Grains of resins or other natural substances that are placed on burning charcoal to produce a sweet-smelling smoke. According to Psalm 141:2 and Revelation 8:4, incense symbolizes prayer. It is a way to respect and honor individuals and sacred objects. The term can be used for both the grains of resins and for the smoke that is produced.

Incensation: The act of honoring an individual or an object with incense. This can be accomplished by a minister swinging the smoking thurible (censer) in front of a person, or in front of or around an object, or by allowing the smoke to rise from a brazier placed in front of an object.

Incense Boat: The vessel used to contain incense before it is burned. It can also be simply called a boat. The name derives from the customary shape of this vessel.

Indult: A privilege granted in exception to a particular Church law by the Holy See or a bishop for a specific length of time.

---

1. *Directory on Popular Piety and the Liturgy*, 8.

International Commission on English in the Liturgy (ICEL): A commission of Catholic bishops' conferences from countries charged with the task of translating the Latin ritual texts into English.

Introductory Rites: The beginning of Mass or another liturgy. The Introductory Rites at Mass usually consist of the entrance procession, the sign of the cross, the greeting, the penitential act or rite of sprinkling, the Glory to God in the Highest when prescribed, and the collect.

Kyrie: Vocative case of *kyrios*, a Greek word meaning "lord" or "master." In the liturgy, "Kyrie, eleison" originally was the response to a litany similar to the present universal prayer. It now forms a short litany addressed to Christ that is part of the Introductory Rites of the Mass.

Lectionary for Mass: The book containing the Scripture readings proclaimed at Mass, including the responsorial psalms, for each day of the year.

Lent: The period that precedes the celebration of Christ's passion and resurrection during the Paschal Triduum. Lent is both a time of preparation for baptism and a penitential time; it is approximately forty days long, echoing the forty days of prayer and fasting of Jesus in the desert after his baptism.

Liturgical Year: The annual cycle of liturgical celebrations, centered on the celebration of Easter.

Liturgy: Any official form of public worship, from the Greek word *leitourgia*, "work of the people." In the Eastern Churches, the Mass is often called the Divine Liturgy. The title is frequently used in conjunction with a modifier, such as the Liturgy of the Hours or the Liturgy of the Eucharist. "The liturgy" is often used to refer to the Mass.

Liturgy of the Eucharist: One of two major sections of the Mass, along with the Liturgy of the Word. It begins after the universal prayer and ends with the prayer after communion. It is structured around the fourfold Eucharistic actions of "take, bless, break, give," enacted in the presentation and preparation of the gifts, the Eucharistic Prayer, the Fraction Rite, and the Communion Rite.

Liturgy of the Hours: The official daily prayer of the Church, also called the Divine Office or the breviary. It is made up of the canonical hours of Morning Prayer, Midday Prayer (which consists of Midmorning Prayer, Midday Prayer, or Midafternoon Prayer), Evening Prayer, Night Prayer, and the Office of Readings. The hours are made up of hymns, psalms, canticles, Scripture readings, intercessions, and prayers. The Liturgy of the Hours is the daily prayer of the entire Church; all members are encouraged to pray some or all the hours, ideally in common in their parishes or other communities. Most clerics and vowed religious are canonically obligated to pray the Liturgy of the Hours.

Liturgy of the Word: One of two major sections of the Mass, along with the Liturgy of the Eucharist. It follows the Introductory Rites and ends with the universal prayer.

Memorial: The rank of liturgical days lower than both solemnities and feasts. Memorials may be classified as either obligatory or optional.

Monstrance: The vessel that is used to display a large consecrated host during exposition of the Blessed Sacrament. While there are many different designs and styles for monstrances, it always has a base so that it can stand upright on a flat surface (e.g., the altar), and a clear round window where the lunette with the host is placed.

Narthex: The space inside the entrance of a church where people may gather before or after liturgy.

Nave: The main section of a church building where the assembly gathers for worship. It is the area in the church building for the faithful containing the pews, distinct from the sanctuary.

Ordo: The detailed annual liturgical calendar that indicates which liturgical celebrations occur on which days, and which texts can or must be used in the celebration of Mass and of the Liturgy of the Hours on a specific day.

Ordinary Time: The liturgical time that does not celebrate any particular aspect of the mystery of Christ, but rather the mystery of Christ in its fullness. The term *ordinary* refers to the term *ordinal*, as in numerical, referring to the numerical titles given to the Sundays of this period, such as the Third Sunday in Ordinary Time.

Parish/Pastoral Council: A collaborative body of the Christian faithful whose purpose is the promotion of the mission of Jesus Christ and the Church.

Praenotanda: The introductory texts in a ritual book such as the *General Instruction of the Roman Missal*. Such texts usually have the title "Introduction" or "General Introduction" and provide important theological foundations and explanations for the ritual, along with norms, rubrics, and other instructions.

Promulgate: Formal declaration that a law is approved and should be implemented.

Recognitio: The statement of approval or acceptance given by the Apostolic See that authorizes certain documents adopted by an ecclesial body, such as a conference of bishops. Translations of liturgical texts must receive the recognitio before they are implemented.

Ritual Books: A book including the full texts for worship, including prayers and directions (or rubrics). The ritual books are originally published in Latin and then translated into vernacular languages.

Roman Rite: The ritual system used by the Bishop of Rome (the pope) and the members of the Roman Church. It is noted for its starkness, simplicity, practicality, sobriety, and dignity.

Roman Missal: The book or books containing the prayers, hymns, and Scripture readings prescribed for the celebration of Mass.

Rubric: A direction or explanatory instruction printed between prayers or other spoken texts of a liturgical rite. The word *rubric* is derived from the Latin word for *red* because rubrics are normally printed in red in the liturgical books. Some rubrics are descriptive, and thus may be adapted in certain situations; and others are prescriptive, and thus must be carried out as written. Rubrics are meant to give structure and order to a ritual. The term is often used in the plural to speak of the norms or directives of a liturgy as a whole.

Sacrament: In the most general definition, a visible sign of an invisible grace, as the *Catechism of the Council of Trent* says. Thus, the fundamental sacrament is Christ, the visible sign of God's presence on earth. Next is the Church, which, according to article 1 of *Lumen gentium*, is "a sacrament—a sign and instrument, that is, of communion with God."

Sacramentals: Sacred signs, including words, actions, and objects that signify spiritual effects achieved through the intercession of the Church. Sacramentals include blessings, medals, statues and other sacred images, palms, holy water, and many devotions, including the Rosary. They prepare us to receive the fruit of the sacraments and sanctify different circumstances of life.

Sacred Paschal Triduum: The three-day celebration of the paschal mystery of Christ that is the high point and center of the entire liturgical year, lasting from the evening on Holy Thursday until evening on Easter Sunday.

Sacrarium: A special sink, usually with an attached cover, whose drain goes directly into the ground rather than into a sewer, found in the sacristy of a church. Its purpose is primarily the disposal of water used for cleansing the sacred vessels and other items that come in contact with the Eucharistic elements.

Sanctoral Cycle: A term sometimes used to refer to the portions of the liturgical calendar pertaining to the commemoration of the saints or to celebrations of the Lord or of the Blessed Virgin Mary associated with specific dates related to the mysteries of Christ.

Sanctuary: The area of the church in which the presidential chair, altar, and ambo are located, and in which the primary ministers may also sit. Normally it is somewhat elevated, for the sake of visibility. It should be in some way distinct from the other areas of the church, yet integrally related to the entire space, to convey a sense of unity and wholeness. It is sometimes referred to as the *presbyterium* or *chancel.*

Sequence: A poetic hymn sung before the Gospel acclamation on certain days. Sequences are required on Easter Sunday and Pentecost; they are optional on the Solemnity of the Most Holy Body and Blood of the Lord and on the Memorial of Our Lady of Sorrows.

Solemnity: A category of liturgical day that is higher than a feast or a memorial. The celebration of a solemnity begins with Evening Prayer I on the preceding day. Some solemnities also have their own Vigil Mass, to be used on the evening of the preceding day if Mass is celebrated at that time.

Stole: The vestment worn over the neck by ordained ministers. It is a long band of fabric about five inches wide. A priest or bishop wears the stole around the neck and hanging down in front. A deacon wears the stole over the left shoulder and fastened at his waist on the right side. At Mass, the stole is worn underneath the chasuble or dalmatic. A stole is never to be worn by lay ministers.

Sunday: The weekly commemoration of the Lord's resurrection. It is both the first day of the week and also the eighth day. It is also called the Lord's Day. Sunday is the original feast day and the preeminent day for the Church to gather for liturgy.

Temporal Cycle: A term sometimes used to refer to the portion of the liturgical calendar related to the liturgical times (Lent, Easter, Advent, Christmas, Ordinary Time).

Typical Edition: The original version of a ritual book published in Latin under the auspices of the Congregation for Divine Worship and the Discipline of the Sacraments. It is from this Latin typical edition (*editio typica*) that translations into the vernacular are to be made.

Universal Prayer: The intercessory prayers in the celebration of the Mass, following the Creed on Sundays and solemnities or the homily on other days; also called the Prayer of the Faithful or Bidding Prayers, and formerly called the General Intercessions. At this time, the Church offers prayers for the Church, world leaders and all nations, the oppressed, and the local community.

Vernacular: The language commonly used by people in a given geographical area.

Vestments: The ritual garments and symbols of office worn by various ministers at liturgy. The vestment for all ministers in the sanctuary is the alb, over which ordained ministers add a stole. At the celebration of the Eucharist, bishops and priests wear a chasuble over the alb and stole, and a deacon wears a dalmatic. The cope, a long, cape-like vestment is worn by ordained ministers over an alb and stole for solemn liturgies outside Mass. Copes may also be worn for solemn processions.

Prayer for Liturgy Committees

We stand before you, Holy Spirit,
conscious of our sinfulness,
but aware that we gather in your name.

Come to us, remain with us,
and enlighten our hearts.

Give us light and strength
to know your will,
to make it our own,
and to live it in our lives.

Guide us by your wisdom,
support us by your power,
for you are God,
sharing the glory of Father and Son.

You desire justice for all;
enable us to uphold the rights of others;
do not allow us to be misled by ignorance
or corrupted by fear or favor.

Unite us to yourself in the bond of love
and keep us faithful to all that is true.

As we gather in your name,
may we temper justice with love,
so that all our decisions
may be pleasing to you,
and earn the reward
promised to good and faithful servants.

You live and reign with the Father and the Son,
God, for ever and ever.
Amen.

—This prayer was used before every session of the Second Vatican Council. It is now
found in the *Book of Blessings* to be used by parishes to begin meetings.